As You May Become

Living into Faith

C. Geordie Campbell

As You May Become ~ Living into Faith

by Rev. Dr. Charles Geordie Campbell

Copyright © 2023

ISBN: 979-888895280-1

Any use of these materials requires proper attribution.

All rights reserved.

Gorham Printing, Inc., 3718 Mahoney Drive

Centralia, Washington 98531

Geordie Campbell
55 Creeks Edge Drive
Saco, Maine 04072
860-878-4197
cgc.pastor.emeritus@gmail.com

In Gratitude

If I had to select one word to express my journey
in writing this book the choice would be easy.
The word is gratitude.

I am profoundly grateful to my family, extended and close,
near and far, still living or on the other side.

I am also thankful for the communities of faith
I have served for vesting their trust and
confidence in me as their pastor.

A verse in the Psalms says it just right:
"The lines have fallen for me in pleasant places."

Indeed, I have been so deeply and steadily blessed.

As You May Become

The title is a phrase from Paul's second letter to
the early church in Corinth. It conveys an
aspirational commitment toward the
the process of growing in faith.
May it be so.

About the Cover

"An Open Path"
by Geordie Campbell, October 2022,
photo taken in Biddeford Pool, Maine.

Table of Contents

Introduction: Baskets at the Crossroads 7

Chapter One: Wake Up Call ..…………...…………12

The Best Start ~ The Moment Is Now
S' that? ~ The Rim of the Day
Jacob's Ah'ha' ~ Extravagant Arithmetic
The Four Things ~ Love's Reunion
Oryoki ~ A Passing Thought
Abundant Life

Chapter Two: Moorings and Anchors 40

As You May Become ~ Whispering Sabbath
The Fragrance of Christ ~ Soulful Burls
Running with Jesus ~ The Shoulder Whisperer
Beloved Little Soul ~ A Simple Song
Useless Worry ~ The Trouble Tree

Chapter Three: Living the Questions ……………..... 69

An Ancient Quarrel ~ The Storyteller
Cana's Finest ~ In a Nutshell
Faithful Rage ~ Dispirited
Running on Empty ~ Soul Pulse
Melancholy ~ Sacramental Ovaltine

Chapter Four: So Many Others **95**

The Balcony Crowd ~ Everyone Belongs
Letters from George ~ A Double Share
I'm Into Plants ~ Stain Glass Partners
Be Blessed ~ Watching Over
Foundation or Fence? ~ Boris Nikolayevich Kornfeld
The Reconciler

Chapter Five: Celebrations and Seasons **122**

A Moth Christmas ~ Mistakes Preachers Make
Gentle Revolutionary ~ Unto Whom?
Be Not Afraid ~ A Dawning Thing
Warm Easter Fuzzies ~ The Locked Room
Henry's Last and First Breath ~ Easter Arise!

Chapter Six: The Other Side **154**

What Time Is It? ~ Nostalgia
Vapor Trails ~ A Different Way
The Other Side ~ Mind Fog
The Long Goodbye ~ I Wonder
One More Season ~ Heaven Only Knows
A Smaller World ~ Mortality ~ The Owl's Call

About the Author **182**

Introduction: Baskets and Crossroads

I once read a compelling story about a rite of passage in an African village.[1] In particular, it involved the Bassa People and the process that adolescent boys are expected to navigate as they cross the threshold to become men.

In their tradition the initiation to adulthood commences at thirteen years of age. As that birthday comes into view, the boy's father and the elder men of the tribe apprentice the noviriate with instruction and mentoring that bridges several months.

When such preparation is complete, they gather the whole community, celebrate the importance of the moment in ceremony and ritual, and then send the boy out into the bush country where he must learn to master the challenges of survival on his own.

The last words before his departure come from his mother. "Remember to place your baskets at the crossroads. Pause by them frequently and listen deeply. This is the where the wisdom of our ancestors will be found."

They all understand that the challenges ahead for him would be filled with testing and fear, mastery and maturity, trial and error. In return he would acquire the skills necessary for adulthood. Intentionally intensive, it would be a liminal and transforming journey in which the boy would return as a man.

Most intriguing to me in this story are the twin images of baskets

---

[1] Nouk Bassomb. "Baskets at the Crossroads." Parabola: The Magazine of Myth and Tradition, 1993, pp. xxvii – xxx.

and crossroads. The first image, a metaphor at the very least, connotes a spiritual repository where traditions, lessons, and values could be made available, handed down, considered, received, and hopefully sent forward.

The second image of the crossroads is metaphoric as well, though perhaps there was an actual place. It suggests a convergence where people and paths, journeys and wanderings would meet; a point of arrival, departure, and return; a setting of discernment, evaluation, and decision.

~

I place that story up front as I begin this book. I hold it close as an evocative reminder of the people and places in my life where stories and values, questions and answers, intuitions and hunches have been given to me.

You will find in the pages to come treasures that others have left in my basket at the crossroads of my growing. Stories, poems, and people. Insight, understanding, and wisdom. Challenges, solutions, and discoveries.

I received these gifts freely, as they were intended, and have shared them in that same spirit of reciprocity. My best sense is that this fits the natural rhythm of life for many of us: we are born and shaped by those who have loved us to life; we come of age as we receive from those who taught and nurtured us; and then, in time, we take our honored part in the process of generativity as we give back just as freely.

~

Six chapters await as you go the full distance with me. They are as steppingstones that have been meaningful to me along the amazing and awesome mystery of life.

"Wake Up Call" offers moments and varieties of waking-up to the miracle of being alive, and the desire to plunge in to all that life has to offer. No one has said it better than Henry David Thoreau: "Only that day dawns to which we are awake."

"Moorings and Anchors" join with *"Living the Questions"* offering two chapters that explore the considerable challenges of living with faith in today's complex world. Reflections, devotions, and poems are of sabbath and prayer, healing and despair, troubles and blessings, laments and quarrels, depression and elation, celebrations and solitude, worry and reconciliation. These encompass the broad spectrum of "stuff" at the intersection of faith and daily life.

"So Many Others" recognizes that none of us walk alone in life and lifts up the many who have become to us as mentors and guides, teachers and healers, family and friends, each contributing in variety to that which has so appropriately been called our "beloved community."

"Celebrations and Seasons" remind us that Christian Faith is one that lives between two great mysteries: the incarnation and the resurrection. I think of these as bookends that hold the Christian narrative together in fullness.

The first is grounded in the very large thought that God showed up with skin on in the unlikely form of a baby in a manger – and then grew up to challenge a world bent on the love of power with the power of love.

The second mystery, the resurrection, extends that power of love far beyond the boundaries of the material world. Just to think that even death could not extinguish the Living Spirit of Jesus; and that the Christ of faith would reach with joy and justice to the whole world.

Finally, *"The Other Side"* invites us to the soul's reckoning truth of our own mortality. "We were with God in the beginning," writes Robert Benson; and "we will somehow be back with God after all is said and done."[2] And try as we might, none of us really understand what that sequence is about. Some have called this "trusting the unseen" by "leap of faith."

~

Most of the stories, episodes, and moments told in these six chapters are from my own experience, reflection, and writing. Where a thought or idea has been borrowed, or the work of another has contributed to my writing, proper attribution provides connection with the author or source.

As the pages turn you will discover that I am an ordained pastor in the United Church of Christ. These reflections are offered with a radically inclusive understanding of the experience of faith, and it will become evident that the life of Christ has been my north star. My faith, practice, and convictions are open to all, and I hope are inviting to you. The arms of God are always wider than we are ever capable of knowing, and the heart of God is vast beyond comprehension.

Though I write as a pastor whose vocation has been largely relational in nature, rest assured that the identities of any others have been carefully protected. In a few circumstances names have been used, but only with permission. I find encouragement in the perspective of Frederick Buechner, who from an imagined spiritual

---

[2] Robert Benson. <u>Between the Dreaming and the Coming True</u>. Harper/Collins, 1996, pp. 4-5.

altitude of the stratosphere, makes clear that "the story of any one of us is, to some extent, the story of us all."³

It is my fond hope that we might each find our way to the baskets and crossroads in our own lives, as they provide us both grace and gratitude in the sacred process of living into faith.

In the fullness of blessing,

Geordie Campbell

Saco, Maine
January 2023

---

³ Frederick Buechner. <u>The Sacred Journey</u>. Harper and Row, 1982, p. 6.

Chapter One: Wake Up Call

Peter Gomes, once pastor of Harvard's Memorial Chapel, was speaking at Northfield-Mount Hermon School. Being of noteworthy intellect he was often asked some rather heady things when it came time for questions and answers from his listeners. But this time, and to the contrary, a young man stood and asked something so straight-forward that Gomes was startled by its nascent simplicity and bare honesty: "Professor Gomes, what inspires you?" Gomes was just as startled with the simplicity of his response, which came almost instantly. "What inspires me is the beginning of each new day. When I wake up each morning and pinch myself to see if I am still alive, I rejoice that I have been given a chance to start over."[4]

~

The Best Start

When I was a young boy, my father would awaken his gaggle of five children for school in an unusual way. He would clear his throat at the bottom of the stairs and then bellow forth his favorite Psalm: "This is the day that the Lord has made, let us rejoice and be glad in it!"

If he did not hear any immediate stirring on the floors above, he would wind-up for a second round, this time adding an interpretive

---

[4] Peter J. Gomes. <u>Strength for the Journey: Biblical Wisdom for Daily Living</u>. Harper/SanFrancisco, 2003, p. 258.

prelude: "Rise and shine! The school bus waits for no one! This is the day that the Lord has made, let us rejoice and be glad in it!"

I would bury my head under my pillow and groan, "Give me five more minutes!" He would respond, "You'll miss breakfast!" I would snark back, "but I don't need breakfast!" Still, he persisted until we were up, ready for the day, and out the door.

~

Surely such memories can become revisionist and even distorted over time. But now, and in the sixty-plus years since, I am so grateful that he started our days like that. Beneath the task of simply waking us up, he did it with such consistent goodness and love. Truth is, I would give almost anything to hear him shout those seventeen words one more time, so precious in my heart.

That Psalm and his enthusiasm have remained with me and are now a part of my story. There is simply no better way that I know to begin the day. So, let's pause with those words, and with what I'll call my dad's wake-up call.

~

"This is the day!" Notice how specific that is! It cannot be mistaken! It's about God's gift of life! Deeply! Presently! Now! And that particularity is urgent, as we only recieve the days of our lives single file, and only one at a time.

Maya Angelo was spot-on in saying it like this. *"This* is a wonderful day! I have never seen *this one* before!"

Dante's *Inferno* tells of a man who was living in hell. Oddly, it didn't look all that different from much of what we see in life. Except for this. He was provided only two dimensions of time to experience. The first was that he was trapped in the past with such gravity that he couldn't let go of yesterday. The second is that he was so grossly preoccupied with the future that he couldn't get tomorrow out of his mind. And so, in the breathing-living-now, he was stuck with what had been, and obsessively anxious about what will be.

That's an intriguing definition of hell: to be locked up in yesterday and filled with anxiety about tomorrow but unable to receive the present moment as it is given. But the Psalm calls it clear: this one, right now, is the day.

~

Five more words: *"That the Lord has made!"* Notice the sequence. Notice that clarity. Notice the prime actor. The creator of our days is God. Still, we get ourselves into a whole lot of confusion when recast the sequence and act as if we are the maker our own days.

More than a hundred years ago Theodore Parker Ferris said: "It's an odd presumption for any of us to imagine we make our days and can judge them as good or bad ones. There is no such thing if we believe that they are a gift from the Author of Life."[5]

Seventy-five years later Henri Nouwen added: "Let's not be afraid to receive each day's surprise without judgement, whether it comes to us as sorrow or as joy. It comes from beyond. It will open a place in our hearts where we can welcome and celebrate more fully our shared humanity."[6]

~

Eight more words bring it home: *"Let us rejoice and be glad in it!"* This part of the verse is called the openness of the Psalm, which

---

[5] Theodore Parker Ferris. This Is the Day. Yankee Press, 1980, pp. 16-23.
[6] Henri Nouwen. Christian Century, "Living the Word", June 6, 2018, p. 20.

most scholars agree is both singular and collective. It's a call to action and choice, arms and feet, hearts and minds - as individuals and as a people.

"But wait," you might whisper. "How can I possibly rejoice when I am waking up tired and still have so much to do? How can I be glad when the list of demands on me runs clear round the block and I can barely hear myself think? How can I feel positive when there is so much pain in the world?"

Paula D'Arcy once asked a roomful of pastors, "What is it that blocks you from living fully?" The responses were revealing: What others think, being right, memories, stuff, stubbornness, anger, old hurts, fear of failure, not wanting things to change.

Then she asked them to literally sit down and make a contract with themselves to break free, to overcome their barriers, and to find the deeper joy in living fully here and now. There must have been some confusion or disbelief that she saw on their faces, so she pressed on. "My friends, it is a choice," she firmly reminded them, "and more to the point, it's your choice."[7]

~

All seventeen words now: *"This is the day that the Lord has made! Let us rejoice and be glad in it!"*

I can think of no better way to wake up each day, and no better invitation to hear as our feet hit the floor in the morning. And I am so very grateful for my father's unique wake-up call which I now

---

[7] Paula D'Arcy. <u>Seeking God with All My Heart.</u> Crossroad Books, 2003, pp. 25-26.

remember with so much love. I hold it as a deep and personal treasure.

I am telling the world: this is God's day!
We rub our eyes – we can hardly believe it!
Let us celebrate and be festive!
We are given a free and full life!
God's love never quits!"
Psalm 118:23-25 (the Message)

The Moment Is Now

A new creature arrived in our home,
blue-eyed puffball of puppy presence,
barely four pounds, one for each paw,
declaring himself the new owner.

Six days in and his command
of the place has expanded exponentially,
charming all who happen by to visit.

The science of imprinting his nascent
mind takes hold, rewarding with treats
the behaviors desired and offering
the steady power of positive reinforcement.

Still, to be honest, it's not all so clear
who is training whom and whether
it is canine or human ingenuity at work.

Best guess so far: it's a good bit of
both, on each side of the learning.

His lessons to date: enthusiasm is
contagious, eye contact is essential,
curiosity leads to more, the moment
is now, and love is all there is.[8]

---

[8] A poem of delight as we welcomed an 8-week-old Shih Tzu puppy, Laddie, to our home in November 2018.

S'that?

I'd like to take a stroll with you around something G. K. Chesterton once said. In my mind's eye, I imagine a bit of a smile as he spoke and a playful frolic in his eyes.

> *"You can look at something nine hundred and ninety-nine times and not perceive it at all. But if you look for the thousandth time you stand in danger of seeing it, as if for the first time."*

It's a curious thought about human attentiveness. It exposes the fact that we can get so accustomed to the world around us that we don't even see it anymore, or we do so with jaded vision or eyes only half-opened. That which is familiar can become overly so, and eventually fall to the fate of it not being not noticed at all.

But then, by grace or luck or a little bit of both, something catches our attention. It's as if our minds slow down and we turn a corner in our consciousness. A pause transcends and suddenly we see something that we didn't see at all just moments before. Maybe it's because the light lands differently on whatever is before us, or a breeze awakens our senses, or a sound disrupts our movement, or maybe "Something More."[9]

~

Scripture speaks of this in a myriad of ways. That's because the dilemma of blunted awareness, of sleepwalking through life, of missing all sorts and sizes of clues and moments, is not only one of contemporary life. It's as old as the hills.

---

[9] "Something More" is a personal way I have of referring to the unexpected presence and action of God.

Jesus spent no small amount of time reminding people that the kingdom of God, the realm of the spirit, was not across the river or around the corner but nearby and within them all along. He said so in seven words: "It is in the midst of you."

Or Ezekiel, many years earlier, who tried to get his contemporaries to pay attention to something burning with the urgency of a prophetic call. "O my people, here is the word but you have ears and do not hear; you have eyes and do not see."

~

I remember a summer afternoon when our young family was on vacation at the New Jersey Shore. Karen, our youngest, was still early in her discovery of the ocean. Apparently, I had not reached my thousandth glance because I was not seeing very much of what was happening right before me.

She squealed with toddling gladness as she watched the ocean. "S'that?" she asked as she pointed toward the Atlantic. Barely glancing up from the book I was reading I simply said, "water." "No, s'that?" as she pointed again. Then she amped it up a notch as she turned with her own emerging conclusion, "big bath!" Then a wave crashed. "Boom!" she shouted. I said, "You don't have to be afraid Kare, that's only a wave." I was doing my very best adult! And then she began to construct a sentence of her own as she strung all the sensory evidence together, "Big bath boom! Pop Pop's Ocean! Big bath boom!"

How in the world could I be so blind as to simply call the awesome magnificence of the Atlantic Ocean just "water" or refer to the majestic swells cresting and crashing as "only a wave"?

Unbeknownst to her, my dear Karen was inviting me, awakening me, to the thousandth glance!

This truth around seeing and not seeing, hearing and not hearing, perceiving some things but not others, is so much the story of life. And sometimes we need a child to embarrass us out of our doldrums, as with Karen and her "big bath boom!" Other times we need something more powerful.

~

How did Thoreau say it? "Only that day dawns to which we are awake." The imperative in that is that such wakefulness is a choice.

Rest it with this. The best of spirituality, the best of life, the best of God, the best of religion, the best of Jesus all in some way invite us to the fullness of life. They invite us to open our eyes, to breath in the air, to heighten our listening, to squeal with delight, and to live into the discovery of the thousandth glance.

We all have the capacity to awaken to so much more of life than we often see. To see the people in our lives for their silliness and sainthood; to hear the many others around us and perceive the cries of human need; to taste salt-air and salty-waves and salt-water taffy; to feel the breeze and watch the trees; to listen to a tender story and offer a friendly heart.

May the wide expanse of God's gifts finally appear for us in the thousandth glance, as if for the very first time. And if perchance it might happen sooner, all the better!

"Be alert! Be present! It's bursting out! Don't you see it?"
Isaiah 43: 19 (The Message)

The Rim of the Day

*She rides along
on the rim of dawn
in a blending place where
light pushes darkness away.*

*She commands
unstoppable power
in sheer cosmic display
of silence and splendor.*

*Her presence
expands, stretching
higher with numinous
spectrum and warmth.*

*Sunrises are like that,
never two alike, as the veil
of night acquiesces and
makes friends with the day.*

Jacob's 'Ah'ha'

Sometimes dreams visit us in the dark of the night with the hope that we might wake-up and see something fresh in the light of the day. This was surely the case for an old friend of biblical vintage, Jacob, and his dream that tradition and history have come to call Jacob's ladder.

Walter Brueggemann refers to Jacob's dream as an experience of holy intrusion. He writes, "the ancients understood that unbidden communication in the night opens sleepers to a world different from the one they manage during the day. They dared to imagine, moreover, that this unbidden communication is one venue in which the holy purposes of God, perplexing as they might be, can come to human beings."[10]

As such, the first recorded dream in the Bible, Jacob's ladder, deserves a thoughtful pause. It was one of those rare gifts of the Spirit, a numinous dream, one that was not just from a restless toss through the night or having had too much chili for dinner, but one that was straight from the heart of God.

~

So, let's start with the dreamer. That's where any good therapist or spiritual director would begin. After all, any dream is first and foremost speaking to the one who has had it. It follows then that the context and circumstances of the dreamer should come first.

To that point, Jacob was pretty much in the middle of nowhere as he fell off to sleep.[11] That's true both literally and metaphorically.

---

[10] Walter Brueggemann. "Holy Intrusion" Christian Century, June 28, 2005, p. 28.
[11] Walter Brueggemann. Genesis: Interpretation. John Knox Press, 1982, p. 242.

The story tells us that he was somewhere between Beersheba and Haran, which is a kind of biblical shorthand for no place at all.

Nathaniel Hawthorn[12] once coined a phrase that fits perfectly here, "the November of the soul." And Jacob was in a place just like that. He had lived enough of his life to know what a scoundrel he could really be, but not so much to have realized his full potential. He had garnered enough of life to know that there was far more depth to it than he had fathomed, but he had not yet the wisdom to live it.

And so, if you will imagine, somewhere in the middle of it all, somewhere in the November of his soul, Jacob had this dream that was so personal and illuminating that it would change all the rest of his days.

~

Imagine: the therapist offers a prompt and the dreamer begins to talk. "So, Jacob, what did you see in the dream?"

Jacob starts to spin it out as he stammers more than speaks, "A ladder. I saw a ladder. It was tall and sturdy, and it was set up against the sky. No, that's not right. It reached through the sky. It wasn't like any ladder I've ever seen. It was more like a stairway or a bridge. It was a moving, open, fluid connector from the ground to the sky."

It only takes a nod from the therapist and Jacob goes on. "I saw more, too. There were angels on the connector, cherubim and seraphim, some were going up and others coming down. They were

---

[12] William Willimon. <u>On a Wild and Windy Mountain.</u> Abingdon Press, 1984, p. 9.

ascending and descending. Something of heaven was coming down to earth and something of earth was going up to heaven. The scene was so free and full of life."

~

By any therapeutic measure it was an amazing image for a man in the middle of nowhere to receive and Jacob knew it intuitively. The counselor knew it as well and so prompted again. This time it was about the message in the dream, the point of it all, the interpretive moment. "Jacob, did you hear anything?"

Jacob now, nearly stuttering with tears of joy and fear commingled, "Yes! God was speaking! And God said, 'I am with you Jacob, and I will be with you wherever you go'."

The therapist again, "And did you say anything back, Jacob?"

"Only once I woke up. I shook my head as my sleeping fell away. I muttered, 'Surely presence of the Lord is in this place, and I did not know it. Surely God is in my life, and I was not aware'."

And then, in what Fritz Perls[13] liked to call an "ah'ha!" moment, Jacob pulled it all together. "That's just it! My dream assured me of God's presence, come what may. It told me that my life is not so far-gone, not so lost in the land of nowhere that God cannot reach me."

~

What an unforgettable dream! It was the very soul of Jacob awakening and reaching out for connection to God. And remember,

---

[13] Friedrich Salomon Perls, better known as Fritz Perls, was a German-born psychiatrist, psychoanalyst, and psychotherapist. Perls coined the term "Gestalt therapy" to identify the form of psychotherapy that he developed with his wife, Laura. Both were well known for their work with dream interpretation.

this was long before any human understanding of a personal relationship with the Holy One had become so much as a distant thought.

Here is the point of the whole story. Jacob's dream is archetypal, that is, it belongs not only to him but the to the soul of humankind. His longing for relationship with God is what all people yearn for even though we may not ever articulate it as such.

So, trust in Jacob's insight. Trust in the holy intrusions that may come your way. Trust in the dreamer's startled wakening, "surely the presence of the Lord is in this place." Trust in God's assurance, "I will be with you in the middle of wherever you are." And trust that this is the inspired word of God given to wake-up any of our sleeping souls.

"I, the Lord, will make myself known to them in visions.
I will speak to them in dreams."
Numbers 12:6

Extravagant Arithmetic

I love when a biblical story fits the form of a free-verse-poem as in these words of J. Barrie Shepherd: poet, pastor, prophet, and Presbyterian preacher.

> *While they wandered in the wilderness, Lord,*
> *you fed your people with the gift of manna from the skies,*
> *bread falling from heaven, new every morning,*
> *sufficient for the day and only for that day,*
> *to be eaten in joy and thanksgiving*
> *and never stored up for tomorrow.*
> *And for those who doubted*
> *and sought to stockpile your bread of life,*
> *their stash turned foul by the next morning.*[14]

Shepherd's words are extraordinarily spare in contrast to the number of verses that Exodus employs in telling us of the same event. But in either form, poetry or prose, it's a beautiful, inquisitive, formative story at the heart of Jewish and Christian faith.

~

Surely you know at least the edges of it. At the center are people who, amid their life's way, feared that their basic needs would not be met. They were tired, hungry, and thirsty; and they were imagining that things could only get worse.

More yet, their growing discontent caused them to become a complaining lot. The story says they murmured against Moses and

---

[14] J. Barrie Shepherd. <u>Diary of Daily Prayer.</u> Westminster/John Knox Press, 2002, p. 39.

against God. They were grumpified if I might invent a colorful word. Some even wished they were dead.

Yet that did not stop God from doing something breathlessly generous. The Holy One did not chafe at their murmuring but instead made bread fall from the skies; bread plenty enough for the day ahead; amply abundant for each and all.

~

I wonder: has it ever been so for you? That fear and fret have cunningly convinced you that you have not enough of whatever you think you need: bread or courage or hope; talents or money or faith or the resilience to make life work out?

But then something, or Someone, delivers you a larger share of the truth; and you find that you do have enough, that scarcity is not your narrative, and that the grace of God will provide in ways that surprise you every time? This is where the truth of our story touches down.

~

A step deeper. Because if the text of the story ushers us to grace and generosity freely given, even to grumpy people; and challenges us to shift our posture from scarcity to abundance; and then encourages us to trust in each day's gifts as enough; if that's the narrative, then the subtext is about the extravagant arithmetic of God.

The red thread of truth woven into the fabric of this story invites us to embrace life daily with trust in God's compassionate grace, with the assurance that there is enough here for now, good and plenty, and more will be coming later.

~

So, let's circle back to the free-verse-poem with which we began.

Early this morning, Lord,
I rise to gather the fresh manna of your love.
Fill me now to overflowing
with the strength, grace, and truth I will need for the tasks ahead.
Then go with me to ensure that I give these gifts away,
that I spend them all as currency for this day,
guarding no store for the morrow,
sharing your gifts in all that I do, all that I am,
lest, like manna of old my stored abundance, turns to waste.

May our ears open to hearing; our hands free to both receive and give; our minds intent on the balance that God has in mind between plenty and want; and our hearts trusting that grace, generosity, and love know no bounds. May it be ever so.

"Good measure, pressed down, shaken together, running over
will be placed in your lap."
Luke 6: 38

The Four Things

Sometimes awakenings come in strange packages and at odd times. Take for an example, how a really good book can bring new perspective and fresh understanding such that it's hard to put it down.

One that has been like that for me goes by the title *The Four Things that Matter Most* and it's worth your time.[15] I tell you about it in the hope that you will experience it as an eye-opener as it has been for me.

The author, Ira Byock, is a medical doctor who directs palliative care at Dartmouth's Mary Hitchcock Medical Center. His practice is almost exclusively with those in hospice care, and over the years he has learned a good bit about life and death and what really matters most to people in the end. Paradoxically, he has discovered that helping people face death enables them to get on with living life more fully while they are still here, even if the time is running thin.

But living or dying, or perhaps I should say living and dying, Dr. Byock would counsel us to say to others and have said to us what he calls the four things.

~

The first, always first, is this: "thank you!" All of us need to find moments to say thank you in daily ways; and not just to think or to feel our gratitude quietly, but to come out of hiding and express it. It's all about cultivating the amazing power of a grateful heart.

One recent morning I wasn't feeling at all grateful. The reason

---

[15] Ira Byock, MD. *The Four Things that Matter Most*. Atria Books, 2004.

was simple. I was getting ready to leave for the dentist to have the prep work for a crown. I was a grouse and not at all silent about my discontent. My wife, Pam, reframed it for me. "Just think of it this way: you could choose to be thankful that we have such a skilled dentist! Or you could appreciate that you are getting a crown rather than a root canal!"

All of our relationships, whether living or dying, are better, richer, more wholesome, and intimate if we would learn sooner rather than later, the power of appreciation and a grateful heart. In Dr. Byock's wise counsel, it's never too early to do so, but it can surely be too late.

~

Second: "please, forgive me." This pushes deeper into the soil of being human. It gets to the gravity of our human imperfections. More to the point: it takes us to the forbidden "s" word of our entitled culture: sin.

Someone once asked me if there was a good way to soften the sound of that. Could we find a way to take the harsh edges off that word sin? Could we adapt it to the comforts of our post-modern world? But the apostle Paul allowed no such margins or wiggle room, and he was right to do so. "All have sinned," he said, "all have fallen short of the glory of God and need forgiveness."

I noticed a newspaper article not too long ago about a traveling sculpture that was making its way through a series of communities in our region. The artist, Samuel Rowlett, called it a hybrid between performance and sculpture.[16] Harnessed to his waist at the end of a

---

[16] Susan Dunn. "Why Is This Art?" in Hartford Courant, August 15, 1012. See also Samuel Rowlett. "Keep it Moving" in Hartford Courant, August 17, 2012.

thick red rope was a 75-pound block of marble. He walked through town dragging it behind him. People stopped and looked. Some asked what he was doing. Others noticed the white trail scratched in the sidewalk behind him. It created some rather intriguing conversation. The whole purpose was to have people consider the weights that they drag through life. He called it "Nothing ever really goes away."

Well, whether living of dying, we all have the choice to try to uncouple and disarm those dragging weights, to ask forgiveness, and to anchor the past in the past.

~

Third: "I forgive you." The power of forgiveness turns on a reciprocal hinge, and we need to ask for forgiveness but also to relinquish and release others by the same power.

A few months before she died, someone dear to me made a last visit to our home. While she was with us, she navigated into a most precious conversation with me. She spoke with an urgent poignance. "It took me a long time to come to like you," she said. We both took a deep breath.

Quick backstory. We walked different sides of the street on many things. Polite, distant, and tolerant are words that could be used. But when I proposed to marry her daughter and take her with me to Boston where I would become a minister, this was just way over the edge.

We laughed as we remembered, though it was a gallows kind of laughter. Then she said, "How could you let me in your house after some of the things I said to you?" And I simply said, "I forgive you."

It was a powerful moment wherein she was able to acknowledge, and I was able to forgive. And I am so glad, *so deeply glad*, that we had that conversation before she crossed over, which she did five months later.

~

And then last but nowhere near least: "I love you." Dr. Byock makes it this plain: "I love you is arguably the single most important sentence in *any* language." And, again in paradox, because of that, it can also be among the hardest of phrases for us to speak.

Gunter[17] was a patient of Dr. Byock. He was a stoic man, German, Lutheran, proud, and highly private about certain things, especially matters of the heart. In the words of his grown children, "We always knew that Daddy felt deeply for us, but he was never very good with words."

But toward the end of his life, he began to look for moments when he would say, "I love you." Of course, the circumstances had to be just right. The setting had to be private, mostly so that there would not be witnesses. But when he was alone with his wife or son or daughter, he would slip it in. "I love you." He even went so far as making eye-contact when he said it, "I love you."

After he was gone his family talked about it. They wished they had heard it sooner. But hearing him speak so tenderly made his last weeks of his life their best weeks with him. Once he began to say it, they were all freed up to say it, too. And as he left this world, they all found a way to catch up on lost time: "I love you."

~

So, learn and practice the four things! It's sage advice from a very

---

[17] Gunter is a composite character of Dr. Byock's patients.

wise man. "Thank you. Please, forgive me. I forgive you. I love you." They provide a perfect platform for awakening.

And know this, deep down: the quality of your life will take a quantum leap as you do!

> *Love bears all things, believes all things,*
> *hopes all things, endures all things.*
> *So, faith, hope, love abide, these three:*
> *but the greatest of these is love."*
> *I Corinthians 13:7, 13*

Love's Reunion

What quickens the heart more than
a wagging tail at his best friend's return?

Soon the whole-body wags, too: six legs
prancing in delight, scampering for a hug

as unconditional affection rises all around
and the distance of a day apart vanishes.

Few have mastered the art of welcome
or the salutation of home more completely.

Rich are they who know such secrets, and richer yet,
who share the exuberance of love's reunion.[18]

---

[18] A poem celebrating the exuberance with which our Shih Tzu, Yofee, welcomed us home for 16 years, 2003-2018.

Oryoki

There is a monastic community in the countryside of rural France that has practiced a faith tradition since its earliest days. It's called The Beggar's Bowl.[19]

~

As the story goes, when an individual enters the community to become a monk, as a last step in the novitiate, he is asked to craft a bowl out of clay. It can be built by hand, with palms and fingers shaping some clumpy measure of moist earth; or it can be thrown on the potter's wheel and spun into whatever smooth and gracious shapes might arise.

The point in the making is not the art, as these bowls will never end up on display. Nor is it functional, as they will not be used at the table. It is rather, a thoroughly spiritual exercise because in whatever shape, size, or method, the bowl is to become a vessel that somehow represents the soul of its maker.

At the beginning of each day the brothers gather for quiet meditation and reflection, as monks often do. Each comes with his bowl. And then, in a liturgical moment of prayerful expectation, one by one, each holds his bowl out to be filled. That's how the tradition got its name, The Beggar's Bowl. Each brother holds his bowl and asks for the nourishment that his soul needs for that day, and only for that day. Such prayerful holding does not cease until all the brothers acknowledge that they have received something of the Spirit in their bowl which is really their soul.

---

[19] The Beggar's Bowl is a tradition that belongs not to one but to many. It has developed over time and is often practiced in Franciscan and Buddhist communities.

At the hands of French playwright Jean Genet, the tradition of The Beggar's Bowl has become known around the world. It traveled far and wide from that rural French countryside to other places and times.

New bowls have been created, and the same sacred drama is played out as humble human beings simply ask for the nourishment and needs of the day.

In the Japanese setting, some additional language has grown up around the practice of the beggar's bowl. "Oryoki," they say. "Oryoki." "Just enough." As if to pray: "Dear God, fill my bowl with *just enough* for this day."

Author Sue Bender explores and expands on this sacred rite. "Just as a monk goes out each morning with an empty bowl in his hands and accepts whatever is placed in the bowl that day as his nourishment, so we can start each day afresh and find, at the end of the day, that extraordinary things have come our way."[20]

~

So, bring it home to wonder within. What does your soul really need today? And what of mine? Strength for a challenge? Discernment for a new direction? Courage to make a tough decision? Perspective to get life back in some semblance of order? Another day of sobriety? Some peace? A song for your joy?

More important: What manner of nourishment might God place in your bowl in response to your humble holding and waiting, and in

---

[20] Sue Bender. Everyday Sacred. Harper/One, 1995. Quoted text above is from the back jacket of the book.

what spirit might you receive it?

    May the tradition of The Beggars Bowl and the waiting for "just enough" - "oryoki" - be ours every day.

"My grace is sufficient for you."
II Corinthians 12:9

A Passing Thought

*Curiosity tickles my mind
with the array of vanity plates along the roads I ride.*

*Each places something
that the driver wants the world of others to wonder about.*

SEAVUE   TWUBLE   WAVEHOG   SCOOBE2
DWNTIM   LOTIDE

AS4NOW   WLDGRL   BKYND   RUTROW
LAUGH   CUPATEA

BCHBUM   KISSME   YIIKES   BKWORM
SUNRISE   OPNMIND

AWESUM   1WNDRS   TINKER   BEPRSNT
THNXMOM   DUNOHRM

FAR2BZY   CBNFVR   XLLENT   LEGOS
CHUCKL   SURFSUP

CARPDM   TRUST   SLODWN   ENOUGH
HEDSUP   UP2HER

AHLIFE   HIOSLVR   SRENITY   MYBEST
BIGSKY   GOTJOY

*Just a passing thought:
What hunch might you receive from me as I drive by?
(Or what hint might I receive from you?)*

Abundant Life

To ride the edge, that is the adventure!

But the edge of what?
Breaking waves?
Billowing wind?
Ocean's surging praise?
The beckoning skies?

Or, closer and more timely,
of relationships that are authentic?
of activities that matter?
of days that challenge?
of a heart that is full?

A ship in a harbor is safe,
but then, that's not what ships are made for!
Why then do I secretly seek the calm?
Why do I quietly look for the ease, the relaxing?
Why do I complain when the wind blows hard?

I remember the words of a friend: "I used to see the good life as a clear and placid lake, feet up, even calm, not a ripple. But now I have a new image: it is one of a sea crashing with movement. Jesus called that sea abundant as he said, 'I come that you may have life, and may have it more abundantly!'"

God, may I! [21]

---

[21] Written on my 35th birthday.

Chapter Two: Moorings and Anchors

"This is what I believe.

We were with God in the beginning. I do not understand that exactly, what we looked like, what we did all day, how we got along, any of it.

Then we were sent here, and I'm not sure that I understand that very well, either.

And I believe that we are going home to God someday, and what that will be like is as much a mystery to me as any of the rest of it.

But I do believe those things are true and that what we have here on earth in between is a longing - for the God that we have known and for the God that we are going home to."[22]

Robert Benson

~

As You May Become

A colleague of my acquaintance tells a story of going clothes shopping as a young boy with his mother. It can be an awkward experience for any child to navigate. And even more, when a part of the mission is to keep the purchases within the limits of a tight family budget by stretching the dollars as far as possible.

---

[22] Robert Benson. <u>Between the Dreaming and the Coming True</u>. Harper Collins, 1996, p. 4-5.

"I think he'll need a size 4," the clerk might say. To which Martin's mother would respond, "Okay, then bring us a 5 and a 6 to try on." She was insistent that whether shopping for shoes or jackets, shirts or pants, "it is always best to leave ample room to grow."

Reflecting on this years later Martin drew this conclusion: "Wearing clothes that didn't fit perfectly can make you feel foolish at times. But it also makes a statement that you intend and expect to continue growing. It's not really a fashion statement as much as it is an aspirational one."[23]

~

That brief vignette parallels my own growing years with uncanny accuracy. As such, I want us to imagine some measure of aspiration that would confirm its truth. What signals might we send to others that we intend and expect to keep growing?

The Apostle Paul stretched such reflection and wondering into the realms of spiritual formation. He wrote the church at Ephesus: "We must no longer be as children, but speaking the truth in love, we must grow up in every way into Christ."

Of course, Paul was speaking in contrast as he often did, urging those of his day to choose one way as over another. "Do not as they do," he instructed, "but as you may become." Or, in another equally curious challenge: "Put on the mind and garments of Christ!"

"What's that," you suggest, "a size 6? No, better go much bigger

---

[23] Martin Copenhaver. Room to Grow: Meditations of Trying to Live as a Christian. Eerdmans Publishing, 2015, p. xi.

on this one. Bring me an 8 or a 10, because for darn certain and sure, I have an awful lot of growing to do to come close to fitting into that!"

And then Paul goes on to commingle not only garments and growth but adds specific attributes of how we are to be in the world as we grow up in Christ. He provides us with his many lists. "Speak the truth in love. Be angry but do not sin. Hold fast to that which is good. Do not flag in zeal. Rejoice in hope. Extend hospitality to strangers. Outdo one another in showing honor. Never avenge yourself. Do not claim to be wiser than you are. Let no talk of evil come out of your mouth. If possible, so far as it depends on you, live peaceably with all." Just a few simple things, right?

He goes on. "Be kind, compassionate, tenderhearted, and forgiving." Now we are getting to the hard stuff, especially that last one. Because honestly, for many of us, forgiveness is one of the steepest challenges as we grow up in Christ. And paradoxical, too. Lewis Smedes once wrote, "to forgive is to set a prisoner free, only to discover that the prisoner was none other than you."[24]

"What's that you say, a size 7? No, bring me the largest one you have. Because I really need to grow into this one, and I'll need ample wiggle room and margins to do it!"

~

Back to my friend. He is far from a boy in grade school now and is retired as a scholar, pastor, and seminary president. (And, by the way, his clothes fit quite well these present days.) He concludes with this insight. "When I clothe myself with Jesus, he leaves me room to

---

[24] Anne Lamott. Hallelujah Anyway. Riverhead books, 2017, p. 49.

grow, which is a good thing because, God knows, I am still growing. I put on Jesus as I would a new an ill-fitting outfit – in order that someday it might fit and be a fitting expression of who I have become."

May our aspirations lead us to grow up in every way to the fullness of the stature and blessing of Christ.

> *"Be renewed in the spirit of your minds,*
> *and clothe yourselves with*
> *the new self, created according*
> *in the likeness of God."*
> *Ephesians 4: 24*

Whispering Sabbath

Every now and again I fall into my soul
as the More of my longing catches its breath
beyond the accustomed pace of my days.

Rest and hope are there, grace and joy, too,
as a wisp of Spirit surrounds and lifts me to see afresh
what just moments before were muted and tangled.

Self is not at all the master of this place,
and edges are not fixed but fluid
receiving what is both full and empty at once.

Every here and there it happens just so, and
time and space conspire as a still small voice whispers,
"Hey, old friend, good to have you back home."

The Fragrance of Christ

Aroma is a curious and powerful thing in life. It can be evocative and alluring. It has the capacity to sneak up on us at any moment and by the mystery of association, connect us to people, places, and times we have known along our way.

An example. All it takes is the slightest waft of misty salt air and my mind is on the beach strolling where sand and waves meet. It happens in an immeasurable instant and my sense of smell fills to overflowing as the ocean's aroma cleanses my soul.

Or differently: freshly mowed lawn on a late summer evening. You know, the kind of grass that colors my sneakers green as I drag my toes. The mere fragrance has the mystical power to transport me back to my grandfather's orchard more than sixty years ago with goodness and love all around me.

It's a potent thing, this olfactory sense of ours. I'm sure we can each find our own way to name a time when it has been just so for us. It's one of the five primary senses we have with which to experience and participate in the world around us.

Lots of science goes into explaining how it works. It's quite complicated. It starts with nostrils that lead to layers of epithelial tissue; and then from there olfactory nerves and neurons transmit such information to our brains in a process called sensory transduction. Ultimately any scent we take in arrives at the anterior olfactory nucleus, which is the memory hub, the grand central station of smell.

This is probably TMI, too much information! But it is precisely why I stopped short when a few phrases in one of Paul's letters captured my attention. It was a missive in which he wrote to the early church at Corinth, speaking about the attributes of Christian life and what it means to follow Jesus.

So, take a deep breath with me, and then another, and catch the whiff of his words. "Thanks be to God who in Christ spreads in every place the fragrance that comes from knowing him. *For we are the aroma of Christ* as persons sent from God and standing in his presence."

What a playful thought! We are the aroma of Christ, reminding people of God's presence in the world. It's quite an artistic standard for discipleship to say the very least. And it ignites my wondering: what perfume or scent might identify us as disciples?

One thought. Far too frequently our congregation has offered community vigils in the wake of mass shootings. They are always raw and painful, but every now and again they flicker with some unanticipated signs of hope.

We recently held such an event in response to the horrific shooting in Las Vegas. As it ended as we left the chapel to form a circle of lament on Unity Green in the center of our town. Once gathered there, from one candle to the next, we passed the light of peace to each other. An Episcopal priest standing next to me turned and said, "I could smell the comfort as we passed the flame. The flicker and slight odor of the ashes of grief was unmistakable."

Another instance. There is something quite inviting when the sweet smell of a home-cooked meal catches our senses. We may still be outside in the side-yard making our way past half open windows, but we know something delicious is being prepared for our nourishment inside the house. Something made with love and tended with a variety of spices.

Linger with that, as aroma invites us to do. Any number of times we have stories about Jesus sitting at table for a meal. Those with him were friends and strangers, saints and sinners, human all the same. Surely, those moments must have included the scent of falafel on the table with fresh baked bread and fruit transmitting a collective anticipation of nourishment and goodness around the room.

One more. Have you ever experienced the fragrance of tears and crying? Wet, salty, close, warm, moist, intimate. They usually arise in tight and close surroundings as one holds another in grief, or rocks a tearful baby to sleep, or comforts one whose head needs a warm clothe on her brow. In sadness and gladness, we all know the sweet-smelling promise of loving closeness.

Paul again. "We are to be as God's presence, spreading in every place the fragrance that comes from knowing him, for we are to be as the aroma of Christ." And the world comes closest to reaching its best, I think, when we take up and follow.

I'll leave it to your continued thought. When is the last time you experienced such aroma and sweetness, edged with comfort, filling you with love?

"Your love is better than wine, your anointing oils are fragrant,
your name is as perfume, poured out in the presence of love."
Song of Solomon 1:2-3

Soulful Burls

I once knew a man in New Hampshire who took to the art of carving wood. "He would harvest the burls from hardwood trees, those lumpy growths that mark maples and oaks and beech trees, and then turn them into glorious bits of craftsmanship."[25]

His art requires a rare and contemplative form of patience. It begins with an attentive stroll through the woods and a careful eye on the trees. A good craftsman, as this man is, knows his trees. He also knows his burls. He knows when a growth looking every bit the wart has beauty and potential hidden deep within it.

Here's a small fact that makes his story far more intriguing. A burl is often harmful to a tree. Even though it may emerge as beautiful woodcraft, it's an outgrowth of cells gone wild, almost as a malignancy can be in human terms. Not to remove it makes the tree vulnerable to illness and disease, potentially jeopardizing or even killing the whole tree. Cutting away that odd lump does the tree good.

Back to the selective process, the woodsman harvests that raw material by cutting away the lump without harming the integrity of the tree. It can be tricky. It involves some climbing skills and a steady sense of balance. And then, when the surgical procedure is complete, it's back to his workshop where he mounts the burl on the lathe and begins to turn it.

The tools he carves with are made by hand and, with them, he draws out the inner potential that was invisible to the undiscerning

---

[25] John Clayton. "His Burls are Top of the Pile" in The Union Leader, summer 1998, pp. 1, 24.

eye. By means of the lathe the burl spins, and by skillful shaving and shaping, he transforms that lump into the most gorgeous pieces of art: a bowl, or a vase, or a goblet.

~

I find his story to be an apt metaphor of the human spirit. Truly, in varied ways, I see God doing something akin to what that old craftsman does with a burl but with our lives. There is in each of us a shaping that goes on, a turning of the raw material of who we are, a harvesting of warts, a sanding toward greater value.

It's a process of redemptive shaping, taking the essence of who we are and turning it for good. And though the thought of being turned on a lathe might not seem altogether comforting, the notion of being a work-in-progress in the hands of God is one of redeeming relief.

~

Hold that thought near-by, keep the idea vivid, and open yourself now to an allegory from the Hebrew scriptures. By close parallel, it's about the creative hand of God turning raw material ever for the good, albeit in medium of a very different sort.

Imagine as Jeremiah leads us to a place called the Potter's House. It is just as its name suggests, the studio setting where a potter works with clay. It's the where the work of formation and shaping conspire with vision and creativity. In this case the medium is clay, and the Potter is God.

Jeremiah can only perceive the Potter's backside, consistent with the Hebrew understanding that no one is able to see God face-to-face. His posture is hunched and leaning, just as young parents at times might lean and bend over their child. The movement of his hands is smooth and swift as he scoops the clay from the bucket.

His feet start spinning the wheel with nascent creative energy. The sacred process is only beginning.

Before long, the Potter's hands and feet and eyes work together with organic vision. A little water to wet the clay and the vessel rises. In a quick slip it is spoiled, perhaps an air bubble in the clay or a thin spot in the shape. But the Potter simply turns the lump again. Pressing it down, lifting it up, forming what was useless into life, as it seems good for the Potter to do. It's not as some inanimate material to a distant hand, rather, as a living relationship, this Potter to the clay: rising, shaping, forming, molding.

And then, in a whisper barely audible, the Potter speaks. "Jeremiah, do you understand? Like the clay in the Potter's hand, so are you and all people to me. Mine are the feet that turn both the wheel and the dust into more. Mine is the love that raises up the best in you, imperfections and all. Mine are the eyes that see the vessel emerge. You are but the raw material. I am the one who creates all that you are and will be. I am also the one who can break it all down only to start it all over again. Or not. Jeremiah, do you understand? I am the Potter, and you are the clay!"

~

Our spiritual understanding takes a huge leap when we grasp that our lives are a work-in-process just so, affected surely by circumstances and choices of the human sort, but ever at the hand of the Living God.

Our perspective is enlarged when we consider that we are as clay to the Potter, or as the harvest of warty wood to the craftsman.

And our grasp of the things that matter most is bolstered when we conjure that we are formed and shaped by God's spirit and grace, a process never quite finished until that final day.

> *"O Lord, we are the clay, and you are our potter,*
> *we are the work of your hand."*
> Isaiah 64:8

Running With Jesus

When I was twelve years old, I noticed my father reading a book, one that he seemed to pick up a little bit each day, often in the evening after dinner, though sometimes in the morning, too. I asked him what the book was, and he told me it was a book of prayers that he found helpful.[26]

Up to that point, my conception of prayer was formed mostly around simple family practices: bedtime prayers with one of my parents, or saying grace before a meal, or learning to recite the Lord's Prayer. It seemed to be something that was important to my elders, and therefore to me as well. But the concept of a conversation with God was not in my wheelhouse at that young age. Not at all.

A few days later and running a good hunch, my dad went out and bought me a copy of that same book. As he handed it to me, I read the title out loud, <u>Are Your Running with Me Jesus?</u> He kindly assured me, "It may not interest you so much right now, but I think you'll grow into this. Some of the prayers will make sense to you more than others. But prayer is an important practice for me, and I hope that you will find that it becomes so for you."

Mind you, this is very risky ground for *any* forty-something year old father to dare with an almost-teenaged son. But my journey into the world of prayer began that simply. Over time it became far less puzzling and much more important. I think my dad was doing his pastoral best to invite me into my own discovery rather than instructing me about the topic and mystery of prayer as it had been for him.

---

[26] Malcolm Boyd. <u>Are Your Running with Me Jesus?</u> Avon Books, 1967.

Over the next weeks I would peek at those pages now and again. The more I did, the more I became interested in the thought of talking with God. And the more that I fed that curiosity, the more I found a relationship with God. Most interesting perhaps, is that I developed a fondness for addressing as God "Ralph" - kind of like we were close buddies.

This is one of the prayers in that book that quickly became my favorite:

"It's morning Jesus. It's morning, and here's that light and sound all over again. I've got to move fast, get into the bathroom, wash up, grab bite to eat, and then run some more. But I just don't feel like it. What I really want to do is get back into bed, pull up the covers, and sleep. But I've got to run all over again.

Where am I running? You know I can't understand these things. It's not that I need to have you tell me. What counts most is just that somebody knows, and it's you. That helps a lot. So, I'll follow along, okay? But lead, please. I've got to run now. Are you running with me Jesus?"

As an indication of just how important that book of prayers became to me, I still have the original copy my dad gave me and it retains an honored place on my bookshelf, as I suspect it always will. I also have three of the author's subsequent books that followed.[27]

In the years since then, I have found others too who model ways of prayer that draw me deeper. Still, the most vivid, most powerful,

---

[27] Malcolm Boyd. Free to Live, Free to Die. Holt, Reinhart, and Winston, 1967; Human Like Me, Jesus. Simon and Schuster, 1971. The Lover. Simon and Schuster, 1972.

most formative step for me was that single book, a gift of the heart, that opened me up to the power and efficacy of a regular chat with God, by the unusual name of Ralph.

I am pleased to report that I no longer address God as Ralph in our conversations (though I do treasure the memory). Most often these days I refer to God as Holy Friend, or Spirit of Life, Heavenly Companion, or Healing Presence. But by whatever name, I sure do appreciate the essence and importance of how prayer continues to enrich my life.

And just to think it all started with that simple book!

"And Jesus said to them, pray then, like this . . . ."
Matthew 6: 9

The Shoulder Whisperer

An experience with the power of therapeutic touch has come my way. In turn, it has opened my heart and mind to the mystery of healing. It has also caused me to reflect on a particular story about Jesus as he encountered woman who was made well just by touching the hem of his cloak.

> *Now there was a woman who had been suffering from hemorrhages for twelve years; and though she had spent all she had on physicians, no one could cure her.*
>
> *She came up behind Jesus and touched the fringe of his clothes, and immediately her hemorrhage stopped.*
>
> *Jesus then asked, "Who touched me?"*
>
> *Peter said, "Master, the crowds pressed in on you."*
>
> *But Jesus said, "No, someone touched me; for I noticed that the power had gone out from me."*
>
> *When the woman saw that she could not remain hidden, she came trembling; and falling down before him, she declared in the presence of all the people why she had touched him, and how she had been immediately healed.*
>
> *He said to her, "Daughter, your faith has made you well; go in peace."*

~

Let me bring it closer. I was experiencing a pesky pain in my right shoulder and arm. At first it was just an annoying nuisance. It slowed me down significantly and I don't like it when anything slows me down. I wondered if I had injured it somehow. I was afraid it was a torn rotator cuff or something like that requiring surgery and interminable sessions of physical therapy.

I took scads of Advil, changed the position of my sleep, and tried to get more rest. I bought the ever popular "my pillow" from the television ads to see if that might help. My wife and I even purchased a new mattress. But the pain steadily got worse. It became an increasingly debilitating part of daily life. Some days it was just plain awful. To make matters even worse, I could feel the shadow of depression and despair creeping toward me.

Without being fully aware, I started to guard the use my right arm. I began to lean left, which had the effect of compromising my posture on the right. That, in turn, brought on a new set of pains due to those adaptive shifts in my body. Nothing brought me any relief. Eventually my doctor diagnosed the problem as calcific tendonitis and referred me to a shoulder specialist. In turn, the specialist gave me cortisone injections and referred me for physical therapy.

~

That's when I met the one I have called the Shoulder Whisperer. She was knowledgeable about muscles and bones, tendons and ligaments, all that one would expect from a physical therapist. That surely gave a running start to my confidence in her ability.

But she had something more, something I would call a plus factor to her understanding and practice. She knew a lot about faith. Though she manipulated my limbs and measured my range of motion, I found her to be one who practiced the power of therapeutic touch. Sometimes she would simply hold my head and touch my shoulder. Other times she reached for the center of my back with one hand while touching my sternum with the other. Often, I could feel a strange sense of warming. It was so much a gift such that I cannot adequately describe.

Over a surprisingly short period of time the pain began to resolve and disappear. She healed me by paying attention not only to my ailment, but also to my whole body. It was amazingly powerful.

~

As my sessions with her came to an end I thanked her for her healing touch. She was softly embarrassed when I caller her the Shoulder Whisperer. As I should have expected, she assured me that it was not her touch that made me well, that she was just a part of a much larger mystery, and that the marvel of the human body was all God's design.

She suggested that along with the story of healing touch in Luke, I might want to go back and read the story of Naaman in the Hebrew scriptures.[28] In the shorthand, Naaman was a man who suffered with leprosy. Through various attempts to get well he happened upon a prophet, Elisha, who told him that he had over-complicated his troubles, and that he needed simply to go and dip himself in the Jordan River seven times. That seemed far too simple to Naaman, and he summarily dismissed Elisha's prescription.

Squeezing the story shorter again, after trying every avenue for healing he could possibly come up with, Naaman wondered out loud to his servants. One of his subordinates posed the question: "Sir, if the prophet Elisha had asked for something much larger surely you would have done it, so why not try this easier, less complicated

---

[28] 2 Kings 5:1-14

remedy?" So Naaman decided to try it. He went to the Jordan River, immersed himself seven times, and as he did his flesh was restored to that of a young boy and he was healed.

~

"Who touched me?" Jesus asked in the gospel story, "I felt the power go from me." Power for sure.

"Perhaps you have overcomplicated your malady," Elisha told Naaman. Indeed, we often do just that.

May all who need that healing touch come to know and trust the One who was heard to say far more than once: "Rise, go in peace, your faith has made you well."

"Go in peace, your faith has made you well."
Luke 8:48

Beloved Little Soul

We fell into a pleasant conversation in the parking lot at the grocery store in the center of our town. It was kindly, good natured, even a bit playful. I had just returned from a three-month sabbatical from my pastoral post and his "welcome home" could not have been more heart-felt.

"So, Pastor, with all of the big thoughts you must have pondered in your study time, what good word will you have for us Sunday?" I teased back, "I only get *one* word?" Came the reply, "Yup! Only *one* word! So, you better choose carefully and make it a good one!"

In that instant, right then and there, it dawned on me quite unplanned and out of nowhere. I found myself responding without hesitation to his unusual quiz. "Then the good word is blessing."

~

The Bible has a good bit to tell us about this notion of blessing.

For one, it tells us is that the desire for God's blessing is a profound human hunger. It's universal. It's archetypal. It goes back to the most ancient of days and crosses every barrier of culture and color, land and language ever since.

During the sabbatical noted above, I came across a book called My Grandfather's Blessing.[29] It's a collection of stories written by a medical doctor named Rachel Remen, in which she recalls the most important lessons she received from her grandfather who was a wise old Rabbi. This story is among those that she told.

---

[29] Rachel Naomi Remen, MD. My Grandfather's Blessing. Riverhead Books, 2000.

"On Friday afternoons when I would arrive at my grandfather's house after school, the tea would already be set on the kitchen table. We would sit down together, and he would light two candles; and then he would have a word with God in Hebrew."

"Then he would say to me, 'Come, Neshumele,' which means 'beloved little soul.' I would stand in front of him, and he would rest his hands on my head. He would begin by thanking God for me and for making him my grandpa. He would specifically mention my struggles during that week and tell God something about each that was true. If I made mistakes during the week, he would mention my honesty in telling the truth. If I had failed, he would appreciate how hard I had tried. If I had taken a short nap without my nightlight, he would celebrate my bravery in sleeping in the dark. Then he would give me his blessing. It was the only time in my young life that I felt completely safe and at rest."[30]

Well, the simplest of truth is that all of us need to receive that affirmation somewhere in our lives. It is essential to our spiritual wellbeing and balance. That's why God spoke to Moses and gave him these words to say, and it's why they remain in perpetuity in Jewish and Christian gatherings yet today. "The Lord bless you and keep you; the Lord make his face shine upon you and be gracious unto you; the Lord lift up his countenance upon you and give you peace."

~

But then more. The Bible also tells us is that once we have been blessed, we need to pass it on. It's not for keeping but for giving away. In fact, the receipt of the gift is followed by the imperative of

---

[30] Rachel Naomi Remen, MD. <u>My Grandfather's Blessing</u>. Riverhead Books, 2000, pp. 22-24.

responsibility. As one scholar says, "True blessings from God do not return void. They are *always* reciprocated."

And so, the receiving and the giving of a blessing turn on a single hinge. "I will bless you," says God, "that you will be a blessing, and that by you all of the families of the earth will be blessed." From the words that we speak, to authentic acts of caring, to the capacity for forgiveness and mercy and generosity and love. In fact, *all* that we do has the capacity to either magnify or diminish the blessing given.

~

The Rabbi again: "Those who bless and serve life, Neshumele, find a place of belonging and strength, a refuge from living in ways that are meaningless and empty and lonely. Blessing life moves us closer to each other and closer to our authentic selves. And so, we need to remember to bless the life around us and within us. When we bless others, we feel the goodness in them and in ourselves. When we bless life, we play our part in restoring the world."[31]

So, back to the beginning. Only *one* word? The good word is blessing! I come to be blessed, and I come to give blessing. It's an equation of sacred reciprocity for all of us to seek and to share – which is a blessing beyond counting, beyond measure, and beyond imagination. So, spread the good word!

"I will bless you so that you will be a blessing,
that by you all the families of the earth might be blessed."
Genesis 12: 2-3

---

[31] Rachel Naomi Remen, MD. My Grandfather's Blessing. Riverhead Books, 2000, p. 7.

A Simple Song

Some stories are so appealing that those on the hearing end might pause to wonder: "I wonder if it really happened like that?"

Consider this one about a man named Karl. He was arguably among the greatest theological minds of the twentieth century, and whether from pulpit or lectern, was revered as brilliant.

More precise in name, Dr. Karl Barth, was held in high regard by his academic peers. He was often sought out as one among them with whom they might shape their own theological perspectives. His fidelity to biblical truth, and his attentiveness to the new and emerging ways of life in his then-present day, were always honored and held in perfect balance.

One evening in April 1962, he finished his last lecture at Chicago Theological Seminary.[32] It was his last public address before retiring. True to form, as his presentation ended, he left enough time for an exchange of questions and answers.

Among them, one of his students asked: "Dr. Barth, you are among the greatest of theological thinkers of all time. You have lectured and taught at the world's most prestigious universities. You have written nearly 100 books. Can you summarize your wisdom and tell us what matters most one sentence?"

Professor Barth was rendered silent as he gathered his thoughts.

---

[32] There is some variance in where this last lecture happened. Some have placed it at Rockefeller Chapel at the University of Chicago; others have placed it at Union Theological School in Richmond, VA. But wherever it was, the story has developed a life of its own. It speaks beyond time and place with authentic power and truth.

He looked at the many who had come to hear his concluding talk. He stepped aside from his lectern. After a time, he cleared his throat and spoke with his native Swiss accent, "I'm not sure I can meet your request for one sentence, but I can tell you with one song. It all begins and ends for me with something very personal I learned long ago at my mother's knee."

Eyes and ears were poised in attention. He surprised every one of them as he began to sing. "Jesus loves me, this I know, for the Bible tells me so, little ones to him belong, they are weak, but he is strong. Yes, Jesus loves me. Yes, Jesus loves me. Yes, Jesus loves me. The bible tells me so."

The room fell silent. Stunned. Breathless. Awestruck. Then this humble professor asked them to sing it with him. He had revealed his deepest truth, touching the heart of his faith in Jesus Christ. And, as the story is told, no one dared a follow-up question to ask for anything more.

"In him all of the fullness of God was pleased to dwell."
Colossians 1: 19

Useless Worry

~

A Free-verse Frolic on Matthew 6:25-33

*It's both marvelous and odd how a single word
can lead to entirely new understanding.*

*Those who study such things translate the phrase Jesus used
in this lesson not as "be not anxious"
but closer to our lives in real-time,
"have not useless worry."*

*In this instance merimnan is the Greek word
suggesting a pesky form
of one of life's persistent realities:
worry that goes nowhere but circles in the mind.*

*Sometimes I lie awake at night and fret,
counting all my "what ifs" and "if onlys"
paying them respect and due diligence -
as if they really matter much at all.*

*And then I wonder deeper, too.
If merimnan is useless worry, of which
I have far too much; what about useful worry
of which I may need even more?*

*War and peace, justice, and joy,
children and the world,*

*equity and grace, mercy, and tenderness
love and hope and kindness.*

*Where exactly is the line that
separates one kind of worry from the other —
the necessary from the useless,
the important from its opposite?*

*"Consider the lilies of the field," Jesus said.
"Look at the birds of the air who neither sow nor reap.
Are you not of more value than they are?"
Have not merimnan!*

*So, teach me, Holy Friend,
to consider what matters most,
and hold me to the useful measures in life
as I learn to let go of the useless.*

The Trouble Tree

I once heard a story, or maybe it was something I dreamt. Memory can play tricks like that, and precise origins can become hard to recall.[33] Suffice it to say that it has been with me for years and comes back to visit with me from time to time.

It's about a tree on a hillside meadow adjacent to an Old Stone Church. The tree was peculiar in shape, rounder than usual, with branches that reached upward to the sky but also that curved low toward the ground.

Because of its roundish branches bending low the tree got lots of attention. People felt drawn to it, and being a part of the churchyard, it became a unique niche in the ministry of the congregation.

One Sunday morning the Parson invited his small community to imagine that their tree had the unusual power of holding burdens. He spoke about how everyone needs a place to off-load their burdens now and again. He suggested that their church was just such a place.

He then asked them to take a slip of paper as they were being passed out by the ushers, and to write down in a phrase or sentence what was troubling them or burdening their heart. And then he did a wild thing. He asked them to stroll outside and hang their burden on one of the low-lying branches.

He assured them that their troubles and burdens would be there

---

[33] This story is of the "where is that story from?" variety. Who was its first teller? The research recognizes it as a story with an unclear history. Time being as time is, adaptations and revisions have given it broad voice and audience. It falls to the credit of "author unknown."

after worship. Still, having the benefit of an hour or so without them would provide a spiritual breather of sorts. He also encouraged them simply to trust that no one would take their troubles, no one would steal their burdens, no one would discover their secrets, and at the end of morning they could go and take whatever they had placed on the branches back home.

Ever since that day, in the roundabout of the region, their church became known as the Church of the Trouble Tree. As that word spread, people came in greater numbers and traveled significant distances, precisely because of the spiritual invitation to simply let go for a little while, and to let God do the rest.

The church of the trouble tree. To be the church where, just for a little while, the weights that bear down could be released; where in the places of heart and mind, a sense of lift could be gained; and where, by the simple practice of relinquishing, a larger perspective of God's providence and care would be accessible.

Not to misunderstand or fall to simplistic notions: this is not all that the church needs to be about, but at least this much. Call it Sabbath, call it worship, call it prayer, call it as you need. But a place where the many things that gnaw in daily ways can be relieved, if only for a while, to favor space for the mystery of life and the amazing heart and benevolence of God.

Scripture bids us consistently to avail ourselves of the trouble tree, except with different words. "Cast your burden on God, and he will sustain you." That's from the Psalms. Or the words of Jesus: "Come to me all you who are weary and carrying burdens, and I will give you rest." Those are very good leads to follow.

So, just imagine we are at the Church of the Trouble Tree today; and the Parson asks us to write something down; and then to hang it on a branch for a little while.

What would happen? What might we write down? Would one slip of paper be enough, or would we need more? Would we trust the moment and the imagination, or would we dismiss it as being somewhat unsophisticated and wishful silliness?

Or, if not on the trouble tree, what do we do with our burdens? What do I do with mine, and you with yours? Does faith play a role in finding the balance between load and lift? And what about the community we call the church? Are there times we simply need a place to let go and let God do the rest?

"Cast your burdens on the Lord, and he will sustain you."
Psalm 55: 22

Chapter Three: Living the Questions

"Have patience with everything unresolved in your heart
and try to love the questions themselves.
Don't search for the answers which could not be given to you now,
because you would not be able to live them.
And the point is to live everything. Live the questions now.
Perhaps then, someday far in the future, you will gradually,
without even noticing it, live your way into the answer." [34]

Rainer Maria Rilke

~

An Ancient Quarrel

There is a story told about a young pastor at the helm of a highly liturgical congregation with very particular protocol to almost every part of the service. For example, just before the pastoral prayer he would routinely say, "The Lord be with you." The congregation would respond completely by rote, "And also with you."

This one Sunday he looked out at the congregation and became frustratingly aware that his microphone was on the fritz. He fiddled with it, tapped it with his index finger, and spoke "Something is wrong with this microphone." And the congregation responded right on cue, "And also with you!"

Of course, the peculiar silliness of that response bears a truth as

---

[34] Rainer Maria Rilke. <u>Prayers of a Young Poet</u>. Paraclete Press, 2013.

old as old as life itself. "Something is wrong with this microphone, and also with you!"

Was that just the fumble of a habitual moment, or, indeed, was there something wrong with him, or you, or me, or for that matter all of humanity?

~

An ancient theological quarrel about this comes to mind. More than a quarrel, it was a foundational and sustained controversy wherein the very basic definition of human life was at stake.[35] It was only partially resolved in pivotal event called the Synod of Whitby in 664 as two opposing worldviews about the nature of life flashed in hot contrast, and one held sway over the other.

On one side was a Welsh monk by the name of Pelagius.[36] He lived between the years of 360 of 420. He was perceived as having very dangerous thoughts because of the high value he placed on all of life as being sacred. Pelagius believed in the deep goodness of all creation which, of course, included human beings. He found the roots of this in the creation narratives, particularly in the opening chapters of Genesis wherein the whole of creation was pronounced as good. To his mind, human beings were and are born in the goodness of God from the first instance, and though they bear the capacity to sin, goodness is the dominant human condition.

On the other side of the dispute was a man named Augustine of Hippo who lived from 354 to 430. He asserted that human life is fundamentally flawed, that we are fallen from the first breath, and that only the power of faith can save us from that. Indeed, to his way of thinking, something was and is wrong with all of us, and all of

---
[35] John Philip Newell. Listening for the Heartbeat of God. Paulist Press, 1977.
[36] John Philip Newell. Sacred Earth, Sacred Soul. Harper/One, 2021, pp. 23-43.

creation for that matter. His argument came to be called the doctrine of original sin, a notion he traced back to the Garden of Eden. His solution to this basic flaw was that the church could provide the means for people to get right with God. In his understanding, sinfulness was and is primary to human identity, and forgiveness through the institution of the church was and is the sole antidote.

~

So, think about this ancient quarrel, and you tell me. Which is it? Augustine: human life is sinful and fallen but can be redeemed through the church; or Pelagius: human life is fundamentally good but has the capacity to sin which can be resolved by grace. Is it one or the other? Is it both/and? Is it possibly even neither? Hear the polarities again.

In one corner, we are all fallen creatures of God and live with the reality of original sin. Our sinfulness is in-born and inescapable. As Paul reminds us: "All have sinned and have fallen short of the glory of God." And as John doubles it down: "if we say we have no sin, we deceive ourselves and the truth is not in us." The only way to remedy such sinfulness is through the institutional means of the church by the remediation of forgiveness.

In the other corner, we are breathing miracles of flesh and bone. Each of us holds the capacity for the most wonderful, magnanimous, beautiful, and mysterious expressions of life that the world has known. We embody incredibly sacred stuff: the spirit of love, the power of thought, the mystery of stardust, the chemistry of movement, the connective tissue of relationship, the miracle of flesh. We also have the capacity to sin, however it is not innate. It is by grace that we can be redeemed, which does not require the institution of the church.

I think that the truth lies in the tension between these polarities. As the Psalmist declared: we are fearfully and wonderfully made. *That's* our human condition. And part of living faithfully is to reckon with that. It's to learn our own capacity for both, neither over-estimating our goodness nor under-estimating our lower ways. And then, to take the high road of minimizing the lesser while we maximize the better.

~

One more thing: the quarrel between these two worldviews is not resolved, the controversy goes on, and it will likely remain a matter of spirited debate far into the future, as long as life endures!

> *And God saw everything that he had made,*
> *and indeed, it was very good."*
> *Genesis 1:31*

The Storyteller

Once upon my ministerial travels I found myself at a Pastoral Care Conference in Arizona. I had never visited that part of the country before, so in addition to my professional excitement, I was quite eager to be among the lore, culture, and traditions of the various Native American communities living nearby.

Knowing the rich history and lure of the region, the sponsors of our Conference provided free time for us to explore the area each day. Accordingly, one afternoon three other pastors and I set out on a road trip to see what we might find.

Before long we happened into an artisan enclave with a variety of folks working in their studios, and a cadre of storytellers and artists immersed in their respective projects.

As I began to browse, I found myself enthralled by a collection of sculptures. I asked the artist about them, and she explained that the carvings were called "The Storyteller" and made of native clay. Each one depicted an older person sitting down with children clustered on his lap. The elder was one of their revered tribal leaders, and he was telling the important stories of his people to the younger ones.

The elder would say, "Come children, it's time." The children would gather around close, and he would tell them of their people. He would tell them about times of glory and struggle. He would tell them of their proud ancestry. He would tell them how to make a canoe and where the rocks were in the river. Most important, he would tell them of the Great Spirit who was the Source of life.

I was smitten. I asked, "Could I purchase one of your sculptures to bring home?" She told me that her collection was not for sale, but the artisan store around the corner had several replicas that might be of interest. She winked as she said, "But remember, a sacred practice and a souvenir are not quite the same!"

~

The image of the Storyteller has been important to me ever since then. It made me newly aware of my honored role as a pastor to be a conveyor of the stories of Christian faith. I am always in some manner teaching, preaching, and telling the essential narratives of our people, the people of Jesus.

One of my seminary professors used to remind us: "the Christian faith is about the story of God's love and redemption for all people. As pastors our responsibility is to tell God's story; and then to help others, including ourselves, to find our own personal stories deep in the heart of God's larger story."[37]

So just for the frolic of wondering: What are the stories that you most value in the lore and legend of Christian faith? What is God's larger story, and how does your small story fit in? What is of core value to you? What are the lessons of Jesus that are most life-giving for you, for which you are most grateful?

"Come and hear and I will tell you what God has done for me."
Psalm 66:16

---

[37] Gabriel Fackre. The Christian Story. Eerdmans Publishing, 1987.

Cana's Finest
A Free-verse Frolic on John 2: 1-11[38]

It's a curious story, the wedding at Cana in Galilee.
I wonder why Mary was so bothered that the wine gave out;
and then, that she turned to Jesus with such maternal expectation?
And I wonder why he was so irritated just before he saved the day
delivering one hundred eighty gallons of Cana's Finest?

Could it be that he just wanted to be there as himself
with his friends in a celebration of love and matrimony -
and his mother, bless her heart, outed him
by putting him on the spot to fix it?
And might he have known that if he did something even gently miraculous
it would be another corner turned toward ever higher pressure to perform?

As for the water and the wine: could it be that in the language
of deep metaphor he wanted to hold the spacious thoughts
of marriage and miracles side by side, as if to say that from this time forth
these two belong together? And so, with one hand he made wine,
and with the other he gestured to the mystical union of two souls?

And I puzzle with the math in the story, even knowing
that whenever Jesus shows up there is plenty to go around for everyone.
But six stone jars times twenty or thirty gallons turns out to
be an enormous amount of wine – and this, the best vintage after
the first allotment had already been consumed!

---

[38] Reflection dedicated to Karen and Meredith's marriage, August 10, 2013.

*More curiosity. Why is it that the couple is not named or described
on their wedding day? Usually the couple is at center, but not this time.
Not a hint, not an image, not a word is given! Could it be that Jesus knew
getting caught up with the particularity of a couple would distract
everyone from the amazing mystery and power of love?*

*These wondering edges are as gifts to me.
The nameless couple could be any couple, the same or different
in whatever ways – it does not matter – only for the miracle of love.
And the wine, what a curious contrast: to hold marriage and miracles
so close as to be revealed together,
one in stone jars, the other in the deep heart of love.*

In A Nutshell

Marcus Borg was a New Testament scholar with a special focus on Christology – the study of the life and teachings of Jesus. Perhaps even more since his untimely passing, he stands tall in the field today, an author and a teacher, a man of extra-ordinary understanding and of deep Christian faith.

I held him in such high regard that I arrived early for his lecture. More: I made certain to sit in the center of the second row so I would not miss a single comment or gesture that he had to offer. And though he spoke to a crowded assembly hall, I felt as if he was speaking personally, as if only to me.

After his talk there was the accustomed exchange of questions and answers. His style of interaction allowed a certain ease as he fielded the many raised hands calling for his attention.

A woman a few rows behind me exuded urgency as she spoke, "Professor Borg, there is so much confusion among many of my friends about this. But can you tell me in a nutshell what it means to follow Jesus?"

Dr. Borg responded with broad understanding and wisdom. He noted there is, indeed, a lot of confusion about what it means to follow Jesus. He added that such confusion generated lots of misinformation that make clarity hard to find – especially in a world and culture as easily polarized as we seem to be. That being so, he recounted what he called the five characteristics that are central in the life and faith of Jesus.[39]

---

[39] Marcus Borg. <u>Meeting Jesus Again for the First Time.</u> Harper and Row, 1994.

"I'm not sure this will fit in the nutshell you are wanting," he said, "but here goes: Be grounded in God. Learn the alternative wisdom of Jesus. Live with compassion and love and justice. Be concerned for others and for the world. And keep yourself connected to the community that gathers in his name."

~

It was clear that the woman who had asked was already well-pleased with what he had offered in response. Still, he went on to expand on each of the statements he had made in greater detail.

"The first is that Jesus lived a life centered in God. Everything he did, everywhere he went, his teachings, his prayers and thoughts and deeds were centered in his relationship to God. There was nothing abstract or unreal about it. Jesus did not ever make himself the reference point. He was always pointing to the larger reality of God. It was a very personal kind of awareness, an intimate connectedness to the Source and Center of Life."

"Then second," he continued, "to follow Jesus is to allow ourselves to be transformed by the alternative wisdom that he embodied." It means taking to heart the counter-cultural and even subversive nature of what he taught, and then letting him challenge our perceptions and misconceptions. It means engaging a process of constant growth. And it means letting him mess with our dearly held assumptions about what life and faith are all about."

"Third, to follow Jesus is to live a life compelled by love and compassion." Those two words, compassion and love, form the foundation of Christian ethics. Not "should" or "ought," as many have come to practice and believe, but compassion and love. And he modeled them as well. In fact, compassion and love are the primary ethics by which Jesus lived.

"Fourth is to be concerned about justice. Following him is not merely an individual or personal endeavor. It is also collective. It means caring about the whole of God's world. It means actively engaging earthly values like equity and peace, justice and reconciliation, inclusively and equality. And it means living these things every day of our lives."

And then fifth. "To follow Jesus is to be in and of the community that gathers in his name." Christianity is a distinctively communal faith. It is meant to be lived and shared together. Some claim that they can be Christian without the community called the church. But honestly, it simply can't be so. Jesus said it best of all. "Wherever two or more are together in my name, there am I in the midst of them."

~

Here is his summary again: "Be grounded in God. Learn the alternative wisdom of Jesus. Live with compassion and love and justice. Be concerned for others and for the world. And keep yourself connected to the community that gathers in his name."

May our ears be open to hearing, our minds to thinking, and our hearts to believing.

"Follow me, and I will make you fish for people. Immediately they left their nets and followed him."
Matthew 4: 19-20

Faithful Rage

It keeps happening.
Again. And again. And again.

Terror. Violence. Trauma.
All through the barrel of assault weapons.

San Bernardino, Charleston, Virginia Tech,
Aurora, Sandy Hook, Orlando.

Tree of Life, Parkland, Buffalo, Uvalde:
the list continues to grow.

Mosques, Colleges, Public Schools, Clinics,
Churches, Grocery Stores.

Malls, Hospitals, Parking Lots, Subway Cars,
Synagogues, even a Bible study.

Lives stolen in cold-blooded hatred,
shattered families, hopes and futures gone.

The heinous suddenness lingers for all of us every day,
not knowing just where or when or who

will fall victim, every breath, only borrowed,
and so abruptly extinguished.

Is there any word to redeem us,
any place that is safe, or are there only tears?

O God: Hear us. Hold us. Heal us. Hope us.
Again. And again. And again.

There is a template of prayer in the book of Psalms called lament. Nearly one third of the 150 Psalms are of this sort. The prayer you have just read is of this sort, a lament I have written in response to yet another shooting, this one in a grade school in Uvalde, Texas.

But best beware. To lament, truly lament, is not for the tame of heart. It is not a calm or peaceful practice. It's to raise the fists of the soul in the face of horror.

The Bible takes the lead. "From the depths I cry to you, O God." "How long, O Lord? How long?" "Why have you forsaken me?" "My soul cries." "Why do you stand so far off? "Why do you hide yourself?" "Tears are my food all day and all night."

And it comes this close. When the bottom falls out, we need to dare and do the scream: Dear God, hear us! And then to scream it again. And again. And again. Though that won't stop the anguish or reverse the tragedy, to lament is the only honest and faithful place to begin.

But then this kind of prayer takes us deeper. Lament at its truest raises our consciousness to human atrocity and injustice so that we can finally hear ourselves. It pushes us to deeper thought, and with that increasing awareness, it wrestles us far down beneath the surface.

Not to misunderstand. Laments are not a "shout and be done with it" kind of thing. They encourage us, rather, to trust the sacred holding of relationship with God as a platform to do more, to ask more, to demand change, and to put our rage to work toward some resolution.

And then this: when we lament, we pray that God will infuse and empower us with the kind of hope that leads us to act, and the will to see beyond to a better day and a better way.

So, to lament: First, "God hear us as we scream!" Second, "God hold us as we wrestle with horrible stuff." And third, "God hope us to the other side." Notice the shift in my language here. I'm using literary license to suggest hope can be a verb as much as a noun.

Nearly all of the laments in the Psalms ultimately turn toward hope. They ride through ugly, frank and straight-forward anguish and then turn toward hope. They turn toward life. They turn toward trust. They turn toward God.

May we remember this essential kind of prayer when the next time - (I ache so to be that certain) - breaks life wide open yet again.

> *"How long, O Lord? Will you forget me forever?*
> *How long will you hide your face from me?*
> *How Long, O Lord? How Long?*
> *Psalm 13:1-3*
> *(A Psalm of Lament)*

Dispirited

*It bears a weighty nuance,
dispirited does, deeply shadowed:
like disquieted or discouraged
but so much deeper.*

*Madeline L'Engle once noted
the meaning of disaster
as "dis" or separate from, and
"aster" or stars.*

*As if to say that an unimaginably
horrible event, a disaster, causes an
experience of distance from the essence
of who we are: stardust.*

*And so, in like manner, to be dispirited,
is to feel an odd distance of body from soul,
flesh from spirit, mind from heart —
alienated from our best self.*

*This is the stuff of lament and a condition
so acute as to want to cry or shout out
in laments that break
the deep silence of longing and loss.*

*Dear God, heal me of this malady so that the cells of my body might
breathe with the stardust of Spirit.
Blend me as whole again, not distant from
but deeply at one with my true self.*

Running on Empty

Once upon a distant day Pam and I were graduate students living in Boston. We had just finished very tough semesters and were more than desperate for a break. So, when the offer came to escape to my parent's cottage on the Jersey Shore absolutely nothing was going to get in our way.

Well, except for this one small thing. It was during the gas crisis of 1978 and getting enough fuel to drive 350 miles would be a dicey gamble at best. Given the shortage, gas stations were not conveniently available as we had come to expect. Those that were open were rationing gas purchases at 5 to 10 gallons, depending on supply. And to torque it up another notch, at its most generous measure our Chevette held barely 12 gallons.

Still, invincible, and somewhat nuts, we headed off, the two of us with our beloved cat Phoebe. We made our way down the northeast corridor counting every mile and watching the gas gauge with clinical obsession. It was a tense ride to say the very least. Eight hours later we crested the bridge over Barnegat Bay.

We were almost there, but not quite yet. I noticed that the little red needle in the gas gauge had dropped beneath "E" and had stopped moving altogether fifteen minutes earlier – though I did not tell Pam the whole truth about that. We were running on serious empty. I kept imagining the engine was starting to sputter. I coasted whenever the chance presented itself. When we finally arrived, we most certainly were running on been phantom fumes.

~

How does the old saying go? You are only young and foolish

once! But more than an adage of questionable wisdom or a foolish story, I offer this vignette as an apt metaphor for life. Because running on empty can happen in so many ways for any of us. Times when we honestly wonder if we will have the power to keep going.

A close friend once wrote this is his journal. "Do you ever feel that your bones have grown weary, and your brain clogs, and your creativity goes flat, and your sense of wonder is strangled, and your marriage is neglected, and your kids grow up before you get to know them, and your doctor says you better slow down?"

He was surely running on empty. He was feeling distant from his source of life, which we all experience now and again. He was having an energy crisis of the soul, and we of the human family are all kin to what that can feel like. I am quite sure that we each have our own best way of naming it as we have known.

~

When I get to that kind of place I often turn to a story of Jesus. He was somewhere along his way on the road back to Galilee. It was noontime, only the middle of the day, which is a shorthand way of saying that there was still a very long way to go, and he had miles to go before he would sleep.

He was weary, tired, and thirsty. He sat down by a well to rest. That thought alone might have some perk-up value just to know that Jesus got tired and weary at times, too. And as he took that sit-down rest a woman from Samaria happened by to draw some water from the well.

Small talk between them led to larger talk. Jesus listened to her such that hadn't happened for her in a long time. Her life had not been at all easy. She spilled out her long and tired story full of longing and hunger and thirst. After listening Jesus responded by offering her something unexpected and remarkable.

"Anyone who drinks of the water in this well will thirst again," he said. "But those who drink from the water that I will give become as a spring of water gushing up with eternal life."

Clement of Alexandria, one of the early church theologians, recognized his own inner need and hunger, just as the woman from Samaria did. And because of this story, powerfully eternal, he came to refer to Jesus as "the fountain of life without which his soul cannot exist."

~

So, let's connect the dots. From the foolish adventure of running on fumes to the Jersey Shore; to the woman at the well; to my friend and his journal and the depleted state of his soul; to that image from Clement about a fountain of life.

I have come to know that when I am running on empty the remedy is almost always grounded in the realms of the spirit. That's why I hold to the story of Jesus by that well as my own today. It's why I take the words of the woman looking for water as mine today, too: "Sir, where do I find this living water?" Most important, it's why I trust in the gentle offer of Jesus: "Whoever drinks from the water that I give will become as an inner spring welling up."

"Out of the believer's heart shall flow rivers of living water."
John 7: 38

Soul Pulse

An old friend called and asked me to take a walk with him. So bright and early the next morning we met at a nearby refuge, a forest of trails and trees and ponds. I knew it was his go-to place to sort and sift when something was on his mind.

Our stroll began quietly as we simply enjoyed our surroundings. But gradually started speaking. "You know I've been in a tumble since I lost my job," he lamented. "It was a terrible blow. I thought it was the worst thing that could ever happen to me. Honestly, I was my work, and my work was me. Then slam! It was done. Over. Nothing left. I was completely bereft."

Silence surrounded us again for a little while. We strolled into the quiet until he spoke again. "The truth is," he confided, "I was totally lost to my soul."

A bit further yet we came to a clearing which seemed as a metaphor in waiting. We half-smiled at the irony as we sat down on the trunk a fallen tree

He spoke easier now, "You have been there for me, and I especially wanted to thank you, and to tell you that I have found myself again. It has taken me some long hard work, but I think I got my soul back."

His experience is completely his own. But the story of losing our souls in life, of feeling bereft from our deepest self, of drifting from our moorings, is one that is universal to all of us, or at least potentially so.

Go back to the ancient days of human understanding.[40] The Hebrew community believed we were composed of multiple parts. "The flesh and bones of our bodies made the vessel. The organs were the seats of thought (the heart), emotion (the kidneys), intuition (gut)."

More yet. "The breath was what makes a person who they are. But the soul was different and more. It was the whole of the person, the unity of the body, organs, and breath. It's not just some immaterial spiritual entity, it is you, all of you, your whole being or self."

The Hebrew word for this is nephesh. And nephesh holds this completeness at the core of human life. It goes all the way back to Genesis when God created humankind, and then, by the power of the Ruach Yahweh – the breath of God - called us "living beings."

Well, that's what my friend feared he had lost forever: his whole being, his entire self, his nephesh. It's a frightening, even terrifying thing to feel. And it's why I was so glad for him as he claimed his recovery: "I got my soul back."

~

Not too long ago I learned of a research project called Soul Pulse.[41] It's based out of Harvard, Baylor, and the University of Connecticut, and is funded by the Templeton Foundation.

It's founded on the premise that our spiritual awareness depends on the kinds of daily activities we expose ourselves to; and it gathers

---

[40] Google: "What is the Soul?" June 16, 2019.
[41] Cosey Cep. "Big Data for the Spirit" in The New Yorker, August 5, 2014. Also, Google "SoulPulse" for a variety of current reports and articles on the research.

data through a methodology know as smart-phone-experience-sampling.

This is how it works. By means of text messages on their phone, people are randomly asked twice daily what they are doing and how spiritually aware they feel. In responding they identify when a sense of connection with their soul seems to be occurring – or conversely, missing.

The database of these responses is growing daily and among the findings: spiritual awareness and connection are highest in the morning; and the activities that increase it are prayer, meditation, cooking, worship, listening to music, reading, and exercising.

Also discovered is that soul awareness is decreased by repetitive tasks where there is little connection of effort to outcome. For example, it is decreased by an over-indulgence of screen time. In addition, it noted that over-watching the news lowers spiritual awareness for nearly everyone.

The technical spinoff of this is the development of an app called by the same name, "Soul Pulse", that encourages folks to mind their souls - eventually leading them to a more soul-centered life. As in my friend's relieved story, "I got my soul back."

~

Here is one more way to wonder about this whole matter of finding our souls again.

A bunch of us were in New Hampshire for a retreat. The convener was an incredibly skilled leader. As we gathered he asked us what was most on our minds. The conversation ran the gamut: from demands of work to matters of family balance; from fears about health to uncertainty about changing economy; from anxiety to worry for our kids; from too much and too little and too many.

After a little while he spoke, gently, kindly, firmly. "I hear of all that tugs at you. But let me ask: when you set your schedule, when you order your priorities, when you make your calendar, do you ever take the time to consult your soul?"

I knew he was speaking to us all, but he looked right at me. And his question is the one that I have been holding as my own ever since. "Do you ever take the time to consult your soul?"

~

When we take such reflective time to pause, and to consult our deepest self, our soul if you will, we may discover as English Mystic Julian of Norwich did years ago.

She found that looking and listening deeply and quietly is essential to our spiritual well-being. We may even find her words becoming near to ours. "All will be well. All will be well. In God's time, all manner of things will be well. For there is a force of Love moving through the universe that holds us fast and will never let us go."

"May your spirit, soul and body be kept sound."
I Thessalonians 5: 23

Melancholy

As a slow shadow rising,
a rumble beneath
low spots in the heart fill in
with the old black dog.

He is barely perceived
except for the empty hollow
and the forlorn face
of dullness and lethargy.

Sky turns flat and disappears
losing every dimension
as clouds and color abandon
texture and depth.

All variances are gone,
no edges, not even slight, as
melancholy sucks the
air from the room.

The old back dog[42]
as has been told is an
unbidden companion,
a visitor to many more

---

[42] Winston Churchill suffered with chronic depression, often referred to as melancholy. He coined the term "the old black dog" as his way of noting the often-repeated arrival of his unwanted guest.

than can ever be known -
but no friend at all to any
until he finally leaves -
only to anticipate the next time.

Sacramental Ovaltine

It was a New England nor'easter, a snowstorm of biblical proportion; and it's a very long stretch across time that my memory travels to get us there. It was early winter in 1958. I was all of five years.

I was with my grandparents at the old gentleman's farmhouse they owned in West Granby, Connecticut. My grandfather, beloved to me, liked to use words like delightful and thrilling and splendid; and the farm was all of these rolled up into one.

So was the snow that was still falling. Snow on snow on snow. The howl and swirl of wind added to the adventure. Before long I couldn't walk across the yard without being swallowed by the drifts. All told, we ended up being snowed-in for three days.

When the first plows came along, the snowbanks were piled so high they seemed to me as white mountains. There was something almost holy about it all, something mystical, something luminous - which were words I did not even know at the time, but I somehow felt them.

Everything looked perfect, glistening, alive. My grandfather and I caught snowflakes; and being a pastor, he also preached a tiny sermon: "God makes every single snowflake different than all the others. That's the way God makes people, too."

Snow brings such moments unbidden, sometimes wind-swept and drifting and wild. God can be seen and known in such glimpses, stirring up the mystery of creation and coming so close in tangible wonder still falling. Still falling. Still. Falling.

My grandmother was not quite as playful or fun about such things at all. "Ye Gads," she scolded, "don't freeze out there!" My grandfather and I laughed as we tried to clear the way in the dooryard, though it collected faster than our shovels could move it.

After a short while we had enough and headed into the house. I sat just inside the door and struggled off my boots that were packed with snow at the top. I shook off the crystals caked on my mittens as I heard Grannie admonish, "Please don't track snow all over the place!"

But moments later her part turned to grace as she poured the best kind of hot chocolate I had ever tasted. My grandfather called it Ovaltine. I smelled the sweet aroma as Grannie said, "Sip slowly dearie, and let it warm you up all the way down."

And I did, and it did, and we shared one of my earliest my experiences of a holy moment – still fresh in my heart all these years later. A sacramental moment: a tangible and visible reminder that God is present and has been very nearby.

"The kingdom of God has come very near to you."
Luke 10:9

Chapter Four: So Many Others

> *"Sometimes, by the grace of God, I have it in me to be Christ to other people. And so, of course, have we all – the life-giving, lifesaving, and healing power to be saints to those around us, to be Christs, and maybe at rare moments, even to ourselves."*
>
> Frederick Buechner

~

The Balcony Crowd

Carlyle Marney was a preacher of extraordinary skill, known most particularly for his creative use of illustration, metaphor and image in his writings, sermons, and lectures.

Two of the metaphors that he frequently employed have profoundly enriched my own awareness and gratitude for the beloved community we call the church.

~

The first is that of a cheering squad. He savored the thought of cheer leaders in the Christian life; and of a footrace being run surrounded by supportive spectators and witnesses. That cheering squad would watch actively along the path of the contest providing shout-outs to hearten those in the race. They believed in the goodness of the runners and wanted them all to succeed. In doing so, it wasn't as much about winning but about supporting the common cause in which they were all striving with their best.

Just listen as you imagine this, and fill in whatever language of encouragement you might have received along your life's way: "Yeah!" "You got this one!" "Pour it on!" "Don't look back!" "Keep your eye on the prize!" "You're in the final stretch!"

~

The second image is that of a balcony, an elevated area from which a better view can be gained. It's an honored place, where a gallery of personal luminaries keep watch from just a distance above.

Those in the balcony hold a certain wisdom. Their experiences and perspectives have earned well-deserved respect, such that they have become mentors and coaches of the spirit. They offer a quieter support than the cheerleaders, sometimes with words, other time not. "I never doubted you." "Well done!" "You make me so proud." "I hope you could see me smiling."

~

Taking it a step deeper, the good Reverend Marney would say: "Now do yourself this very important favor. Every now and again, step back from the heat of the race and look around; or gaze up to the balcony above and see those steady and precious faces."

Mothers and fathers, sisters and brothers, children and grand and great grandchildren, partners, and spouses. These are the ones who invested their love and lives for us. We hold a special place for them at the eternal table in our hearts. They have been the shapers of who we have grown to be and become. "Blow them a kiss," Dr. Marney would say. "Throw them a hug. Toss them a thumbs up or a smile. They are the ones who we can never quite thank enough."

And then this, which Marney was heard to say far more than once over his years of teaching and preaching: "Give them a grateful nod and a wave, because they are your saints! Some you never even knew of, and others who are dear to your heart. It is good to give thanks."

~

Honestly, we would all be remiss not to simply stop now and again and say, "thank you, and you, and you, and . . ." The list is long, beloved, motley, and rich.

It may take some time to acknowledge all of them. But please don't wait too long.

"Therefore, since we are surrounded by so great a cloud of witnesses let us run with perseverance the race that is set before us, looking to Jesus, the pioneer and perfecter of our faith."
Hebrews 12: 1-2

Everyone Belongs

Something purrs as pieces of a jigsaw puzzle

slip into place

and the sensation of fit is found

among   cardboard

cutouts,   seemingly   random,

creating   a larger   picture   with

order and form,   boundary and definition,

color,   shape,   and expression,

as if to say   in a whisper   of searching relief:

in God's time,

every piece belongs,

nothing is ever wasted,

nothing is ever left over.

Letters from George

George Bowers was the Senior Pastor at Christ Lutheran Church in Lewisburg, Pennsylvania where my wife Pam grew up. He was an inspired man, highly energetic, and wonderful with youth. In every way, he became one of the most important people in Pam's life.

Pam struggled as a child. Through various sequence of earaches and multiple surgeries, she became almost entirely deaf when she was in the second grade. Needless to say, she was terrified as her world suddenly became muted and silent.

As grace would have it, Dr. Bowers became aware of this, took special interest, and reached out to her. One of those instances was on a hayride. He was on an autumn outing with the youth group from his congregation. The kids were playful, even a bit unruly, tossing hay at one another across the center of the wagon. Some of the flying straw landed in Pam's eye. Her vulnerability of not hearing mixed into the moment and she was overwhelmed as she began to cry. Dr. Bowers crossed from where he had been sitting amid the hay and sat next to her, providing the reassurance that all would be okay. Pam remembers that experience as one of the most formative moments in her young life.

Later that year, it was George Bowers who saw to it that Pam would learn sign-language. That reopened her world as she discovered a new way to communicate. Later again, he formed a specialized ministry to the deaf in their congregation, which eventually led to him initiate a sign language choir at the church. He led that choir which provided Pam yet another opportunity to overcome her auditory challenges.

Through those young years, it was Dr. Bowers who consistently journeyed the extra mile for Pam, ensuring that she was never left out. His example and faith provided a powerful and personal witness to her and shaped her early and emerging life toward Christ.

Five years later when the time came for Dr. Bowers to accept the call to another a congregation in Roanoke, Virginia he continued his active outreach to her. They became pen-pals. He wrote wonderful letters to her, encouraging epistles of faith. He not only wrote of his own convictions in those letters, but for Pam, his very life became a living letter of faith to her.

To this day, Pam still has those letters tucked away in a thick manilla folder in her desk. They have followed everywhere she has lived in the years since: from Pennsylvania to Boston; from Vermont to Connecticut; and now to Maine. Those letters are among her most dearly prized possessions.

It often happens that the primary gift of faith is transacted like that. Whether in person or by letter, by word or deed, a seed is planted and cultivated as someone brings to bear the grace of God and the love of Jesus for another.

~

I want us to stretch beyond the edges of Pam's story to realize that this gift of being as a living letter of Christ - others to us, and us to others – is integral to what it means to call ourselves Christian.

This is what Paul was getting at when he suggested that we become as letter-bearers, one to each other, and that our very lives become as virtual letters of Christ.

By Paul's hand: "You are yourselves letters of recommendation written not on tablets of stone, but on tablets of the heart."

~

A postscript to Pam's story. Quite beyond any clinical explanation by her doctors or specialists, Pam's hearing did return later in her grade school years. Some would use the word miraculous in describing the way that her life turned around. She went on to sing in the middle school chorus and play the flute the high school band. No one ever could have guessed that only a few seasons earlier she was deaf.

Pam's adult years led to a vocation of helping others to heal. The empathy, compassion, and living example that George Bowers provided endured for her and through her. She became a social worker with a special focus on gerontology. A few tears later she became a registered nurse, able to hear the barely perceptible measures of blood pressures just fine. Later yet again she became a Medical Family Therapist where her skill of listening carefully to the life stories of others brought them to well-being and healing.

I have absolutely no doubt that the influence of Dr. Bowers has been, is now, and will always be as the spiritual compass of her life. His life was as a letter of Christian love, written on his own heart and delivered in so many lasting ways to hers.

"Keep on doing, as you have learned and received and heart and seen in me, and the God of peace will be with you."
Philippians 4:9

A Double Share

A vivid story in Hebrew scripture tells
of two servants of Yahweh and the day of their parting.
Elijah, the older one by nearly a generation, was in his last days,
and Elisha, the younger whom he had mentored,
were strolling for what would be their last afternoon chat.

Various sequence of legend and miracle overflowed
as they walked along the Jordan: Elijah's deep trust in God,
Elisha's insistence that he would not ever leave his teacher's side;
something of a whirlwind that would carry Elijah
to heaven by chariot, and a mantle that would fall to the ground.

Just then Elijah asked his protégé, "What might I do
for you before I am taken from you?" Elisha was quick,
"Let me inherit a double share of your spirit." The elder spoke,
"You have asked a hard thing." Still, before long
the chariot arrived as promised, and the older one ascended.

It was unfolding as if God had intended it all along.
As he was lifted-up Elijah's mantle fell from his holding
and drifted to the ground beneath where Elisha still stood.
He picked it up and immediately felt its mystical power.
And all who watched said, "The spirit of Elijah now rests on Elisha."

How lucky are those of us who have had mentors
and teachers, pastors and coaches, parents and friends - unbidden,
unexpected, even at times unknown:
those who have shown us the path,
who by the Spirit of God have left behind a double share,

and dropped a mantle at just the right time,
in exactly the right place.⁴³

---

⁴³ This biblical reflection was written in deep gratitude to Tuck Gilbert who was a mentor par excellence from my early days in seminary to the cusp of my retirement forty years later. I offered these words as a portion of his eulogy in June 2018. Shortly after his memorial service, I received Tuck's stole, the mantle of his vocation, from his family in appreciation for the unique role that he played in my life and ministry.

I'm Into Plants

I was a student minister at the Trinitarian Congregational Church in Concord, Massachusetts when this lovely encounter came my way. I remember as if it happened yesterday.

It was my first day at Tricon and I was nervous more than I can aptly describe, still so new at this pastoral gig. A rather round-faced man came up to me at coffee hour full of encouragement. "Glad to have you with us," he said, "I like your speaking voice. It's very clear and your enunciation is excellent. I've done a good bit of public speaking myself and I can recognize talent when I see it."

I thanked him for his enthusiasm and support. We bantered with a bit of small talk fitting for the context. I engaged the conversation more by asking what he did for a living. "Oh, I'm into plants," he said quietly with a smile. It almost sounded apologetic. After a short while our conversation found its comfortable end and we both departed.

Later that week I saw him again. This time I was turning the channels on our television. There was that pleasant face and smile again! The man who had been so unassuming in telling me that he was into plants was Jim Crockett – a name very well-known at the time for his prime-time TV Show "Crockett's Victory Garden."

And later again that week I was at the Chestnut Hill Mall and strolled into a Walden Bookstore. Right as I entered, positioned at sightline so as not to miss it was his latest book[44] by the same title as

---

[44] James Underwood Crockett. <u>Crockett's Victory Garden</u>. Little Brown and Company, 1977.

his TV show. I picked it up and looked eagerly through the pages. The clerk at the store noticed my interest and made sure to tell me that the author would be doing a book signing on Saturday morning if I might line to meet him.

The next week at church I apologized to him six ways to Sunday and probably more. I stammered, "I am so sorry that I did not know who you are. Even more, I'm embarrassed that I did not pick up on your clue to me that you are into plants!"

His kindness and humility spoke truly from the heart. "I could tell you didn't recognize me. Thank you for that gift. It was so refreshing. Matter of plain fact I enjoyed it. It made my day. Besides the fame I find in the public eye, I would rather you just know me as Jim."

Friends, that's how the heart of God would rather know each of us, and have us know one another, too! Walk humbly. Be unpretentious. Live unassuming.

"What does the Lord require of you?
Do justice, love kindness, and walk humbly."
Micah 6: 8

Stained Glass Partners

A story is told of a church down south whose sanctuary is adorned with unusually beautiful stained-glass windows.[45] They are colorful and bright and refract the sun's light with warmth and spiritual presence. Honestly, for most of the members, being there just to see the dance of color and light is nearly worship enough.

One Sabbath day a visitor happened in for the morning service and fell under the numinous spell of those windows. In fact, he spent the whole hour simply looking at each one of them from the vantage point of his pew.

There were twelve in all, each depicting some of the great stories along faith's way. The prodigal son was there, and Mary was kneeling in reverence before an angel. An adult Jesus was holding a shepherd's crook; in another a shepherd was dazzled by a Bethlehem star; and in another the sea calmed down around a storm-tossed boat. You get the idea, each of these stained-glass windows told some part the larger God-story of redemption and hope.

As service ended the man went for a closer look. He noticed lots more detail in the stained-glass panels, and that each of the windows was dedicated to someone's memory on brass nameplates. He assumed, of course, that these were noteworthy benefactors of that particular church: pastors and deacons and leaders of such variety.

As he left, he asked the pastor at the door about the windows and the names. The pastor explained that they are of folks unknown to

---

[45] This story has been told and adapted in varied forms. The author of the original version was probably Fred Craddock.

anyone in that church. Apparently, the windows had been purchased at an auction. They had been salvaged from a church that had fallen into disrepair, and subsequently had been torn down.

The minister went on, now joined by a woman who happened to be a deacon, "We thought about taking the names off so as not to confuse anyone, just as we have done with you this morning." The woman finished the preacher's train of thought, "But then we figured that it was important to keep the names. It reminds us of every time we gather that the church is far more than just us."[46]

~

That is so very true. The church is fathoms larger, immeasurably, uncountably more than any single one of us. We are all a part of it for sure, but none of us is the whole of it; though admittedly at times, fallible and foolish people have elevated themselves above all the rest.

But there are, thank goodness and God, names, and faces and people that all have a hand and a part in the story who remind us that the church is always bigger than any individual or time.

Some of these others are quite personal to us, kind of our own gallery of saints. Some are still living, and some have gone the way of all the earth. Some bear our own names, at least in part, and others have taught or shown us the goodness of life and the power of love. Some tenderly rocked us to sleep, and others gave us a serious wake-up call along the way.

~

The writer of Hebrews, whose name is not known to us perhaps

---

[46] Martin Copenhaver. To Begin at the Beginning. Pilgrim Press, 2002, p. 98.

intentionally, calls these others a great cloud of witnesses, imagining a living presence all around us, every waking and sleeping moment.

A long parade of names only begins to account for them: Abel and Enoch and Noah; Abraham and Sarah; Isaac and Jacob and Esau and Joseph and Moses and Rahab; Ruth and Lydia and Gideon and Barak and Samson and David and Samuel.

If we stopped to pay attention, we would find that it is a motley and mixed-up crowd, just like all the rest of us. But these are among our forebear's and cousins and the company to whom we belong. These are those who, in their own time, were exemplars and guides in faith.

And this, too, we are told: "these all died in faith, not having received what was promised, but having greeted it from afar, though time fails to tell of them all."

~

We do not ever really walk alone in this life. There are a great many others, named and not, who share the road with us. And there are many more of whom we have not even a hunch. "Known and unknown, seen and unseen," as a famous prayer captures it. Some are here today in body and others only by blessing of spirit. Some are cast in leaded glass, and others simply in the whisper of the Spirit.

> *"These all died in faith without having received the promises,*
> *but having greeted it from a distance . . ."*
> *Hebrews 11:13*

Be Blessed

He appeared as if out of nowhere,
dressed entirely in distinctive black
complementing his mustache and beard.

His presence was reassuring as he asked
in eternally forever moments, "What happened?"
"Is he still breathing?" "Is help on the way?"

A close friend lay dying on the street
in the city he liked to call his hometown.
"911, please as fast as you can,

Broadway and West 63rd. 78 years old."
And then, also out of nowhere, a cardiologist
erupted into action from the crowd.

Sounds of sirens in the distance came closer.
One ambulance came, and then another
delivering all of the intervention that a

timeless trauma could possibly hold.
"Roosevelt Hospital. Tenth and 59th."
The ambulance raced away.

Soon the streets filled with cars again

as the momentary community of bystanders
dispersed and moved on.

The man in black simply said "Be blessed"
as he slipped into the anonymity
of a misty damp Manhattan evening.[47]

---

[47] A terrifying evening but one from which my friend eventually recovered. He had suffered full cardiac arrest. Had it not been for the random stranger calling for help and the intervention of an unknown cariologist in the crowd, he probably would not have survived.

Watching Over

*It was chilly at the gravesite,
damp and translucent
as a thin veil of fog mystified
the reason we had come.*

*Death does not schedule
with concern for weather,
and the mist that morning
did not delay our need
to bring a loved one to rest.*

*Ancient words were spoken,
voices calling out to God
as the goodness of a shepherd.*

*A man watched from the hillside,
appearing oddly surreal to me
as we must also have seemed.*

*He offered a wave, barely slight,
but enough to make me wonder:
who is this who watches over
such eternal moments?*

*When all was done, I approached
to ask his purpose. He kindly said,
"You do not know me, but I deeply
appreciate the work that you do."*

*When I turned to look again,
I saw only his backside through the mist,
and the hillside and the grave, too;
the ground still opened, still fresh,
as the fog began to lift.*

Foundation or Fence?

Two stories commingle in my thoughts about diversity, inclusion, and the wide arms of God, made known to all of us in so many ways. They each speak with their own poignance and power.

~

I once attended an inspiring and panel discussion at our local synagogue. The presenters were three mothers - Suzanne who is Christian, Ranya who is Muslim, Priscilla who is Jewish. Each of them was thrust into a tumultuous faith crisis on September 11, 2001. Each found herself that day and in the months that followed in a fearful tumble about her family's beliefs and their safety in the violent realities in the world.

That vulnerability initiated the nascent steps of a journey that formed among the three of them, though they knew little of one another at the time. Mother's feeling vulnerable for their families and children can be a powerful magnet as it was for them. But their group quickly grew and has come to be known as the Faith Club.

The three of them wrote a book together by that same title in which they discovered the urgency of open dialogue among different communities, faiths, and individuals.[48] It became as a burning fire in them. As these three set out on tour promoting their call to dialogue, they opened a platform of conversation across the land about interfaith understanding.

At one of those gatherings that I attended Priscilla said: "What it all comes to is doing the hard work of love. Very hard work. It has

---

[48] Rayda Idiby, Suzzanne Oliver, Priscilla Warner. The Faith Club. Simon and Schuster, 2007.

not been easy." And then Ranya leaned toward her microphone: "But we honestly believe it's the only way we will ever have a world of peace and hope."

I was captured in urgency and clarity as these three women opened my heart, mind, and eyes, as they did for everyone in the room - which was a large public venue filled to overflowing. That's the first story.

~

Hold that vignette and add in another conversation about essentially the same urgent dilemma.

It happened in a group with seventeen very diverse people. We were as young as 36 and as seasoned as 75. We were married and single, conservative and liberal, activist and evangelical. Some were gay and others straight. We were Lutheran, UCC, Episcopalian, New Age, Jewish, Roman Catholic, Methodist, and Presbyterian.

It was a session called Theological Reflection offered at a nearby Spiritual Life Center, and we were focusing on the reality of suffering. We were just beginning the discussion. At first, we were filled with hesitation, but before long we all discovered that there was no lack of opinion or comment among us.

One person spoke, and then another, and then another. A story, some silence, some nodding heads. But then someone made a few rather unusually harsh comments about what God does or doesn't do in the world. Almost instantly, tensions began to build. It was palpable. Our differences flared as raw and defining edges. We had broken our polite veneer of tolerance and as it seemed to vanish, we were left suspended in an awkward silence.

A Lutheran pastor named David spoke in non-anxious and confident tones. "What is most important to me in understanding you is whether I allow my faith to be a foundation or a fence. When I trust it as my foundation, it gives me a place to stand and enables me to open my mind and heart and to listen to you, different as we are. But when my faith becomes a fence, when I let it become the defining point of difference between us, it becomes a barrier and a wall. In my better moments my faith is that foundation. In my lesser moments, it becomes that fence."

As in the first story, I was wrapped in attention and clarity, urgency and hope as the seventeen of us opened our hearts, minds, and eyes. We were so much smaller in this second setting but moved every bit the same as we sought to understand ourselves and others in the spirit of faith seeking understanding.

~

I found each of these conversations tremendously helpful as I sort and sift my own perspective and faith. One highlights the hard work of love and how essential it is to increase our understanding. The other differentiates between the fences that separate us and the foundations that support us. Both reveal the necessary work that cannot be accomplished alone, in silos, or in silence.

My memory of both events and the vivid honesty shared combine and tell me something about how vital, urgent, and critical their truth is for the future of this God-so-loved-world and our diverse understandings of faithfulness.

"God has made of one blood all people of the earth."
Acts 17:26

Boris Nikolayevich Kornfeld

We never fully know how we influence others along their way. Just as true, we are most often unaware of the ways that others have influenced us. "It's something he did that I can't ever forget," we might whisper quietly. Or "she had an effect on me that I am still growing to understand." Or "my life has never been the same."

~

Boris Nikolayevich Kornfeld was a medical doctor.[49] He lived in the Soviet Union in the days when people were imprisoned for all kinds of non-reasons. His lot in life was to work in a prison, giving medical aid to prisoners in the infirmary. Essentially, he himself was a prisoner, incarcerated to provide medical care to other prisoners.

One night Dr. Kornfeld treated an inmate who was dreadfully sick. In fact, the man was in such a state that the doctor was certain he would die before the next dawn and so he kept vigil through the night at his bedside.

During the darkest watch of the night, partly to keep himself awake and partly to keep his patient oriented, Kornfeld told the story of his faith. He recounted how he had been compelled by the power of Jesus, and how this had caused his conversion from atheism to Christianity. As the patient became more fully conscious, he knew that he was hearing an incredibly personal confession of faith.

Within the day the Dr. Kornfeld was arrested and executed for his

---

[49] Google: Alexander Solzhenitsyn, "What I Learned in the Gulag." Source: Internet Modern History Sourcebook. The Sourcebook is a collection of public domains materials and permits the use of certain texts for introductory classes in Modern European and World History. Excerpts from The Gulag Archipelago.

crime of speaking about Jesus to his patients.

It could have ended there, but it didn't. Because against all odds the patient recovered. He could never forget the care of the doctor or the long night of so personal a story. In fact, the essence of Dr. Kornfeld's faith became as a leaven in the loaf of that patient's life. It became profoundly transformative.

The patient's name was Alexander Solzhenitsyn, and he recalls that single night as one of the most profound experiences in his entire life, leading to his conversion from Judaism to Christianity. His life was literally saved, and his soul redirected, by that doctor's night-time telling.

~

It honestly happens like that, every now and then, every here and there. Someone just sprinkles some leaven in our loaf. Or we plant some seeds in the soul of another. Just as Jesus said, it can have transforming power. The kingdom of God is like that: as a seed secretly planted, or the hidden measure of yeast that brings the bread to rise.

'It is like the yeast that a woman took and mixed in with three measures of flour until all of it was leavened.
Luke 13:21

The Reconciler

There are times when understanding things of the theological variety can best be accomplished through a story of life. I suspect that's why Jesus chose to teach so consistently in parables. It is also why I tell this single story.[50]

~

There was once a merchant who had twin sons. They were as close as close could be, these two, identical in nearly every way, born of the same flesh, cut from the same cloth. They dressed alike, looked alike, went to the same schools, developed the same interests, had the same friends, did the same things. As they rode the years through childhood into adolescence and even older, they were, as the adage would coin it, "just like peas in a pod!"

By and by their father died and the two boys, now men, were left to manage the family store together. This was nothing all that new because they had shared in that all their lives. They knew the business in their bones and worked as they had always done, side by side. And so it was, happy and together, that their little enterprise became known as The Brother's Store.

One morning a customer came in to make a small purchase. The brother who waited on him received a dollar bill in payment, placed it on top of the cash register, and then cordially walked the man back out to the sidewalk. When he returned the dollar was gone. He turned to ask his brother where the dollar was, and he replied that he knew nothing about it. "That's strange," the other said, "I distinctly

---

[50] John Claypool. The Preaching Event. Word Books, 1980, pp. 35-40. I am grateful to the Rev. Dr. John Claypool who told the story of the reconciler in its presumptive original form and has generously allowed for its adaptation by many others.

remember placing the bill on the resister, and no one else has been in the store but you."

Had the matter dropped at that point - an insignificant issue by any real measure - nothing more would have happened. But it did not stop. It went on.

The next day, now with deeper suspicion, the first brother brought it up again. "Are you sure you didn't take that dollar bill?" And the other brother, quickened by anger now, hurt by the lack of trust, defensive deep down, snapped back, "I already answered that question! I don't know anything about your foolish dollar bill!"

The distance grew wider and wider and wider. Charges and countercharges grew up between them. Mutual friends got drawn in - some even took sides. Still, it did not stop. For the love of being right it went on, and their pain grew, and their misunderstanding – once very small became larger than could ever make sense.

After a time, things got so bad that they dissolved the business. It was no longer called The Brother's Store. They divided the space in half, put up an impenetrable wall, and began to live separate and increasingly bitter lives. Silently, each brother hoped that at some point the other would concede to his dishonesty. But it was not to be. Twenty years passed and they did not speak.

Well, one day a car with out-of-state license plates pulled up in front of the store that now housed the two brothers separately. A stranger got out and went in to one side. He spoke right up: "I hope you can help me. I am here to settle a score. Twenty-some years ago, I was out of work. I was drifting from place to place. I had absolutely no money and had not eaten for days. I was desperate. As

I walked down the alley behind your store, I looked in and saw a single dollar bill on top of your cash register. No one seemed to be around, so I took it. It has haunted me ever since. I am here to repay you whatever is appropriate."

The old-man-of-a-brother crumbled to tears as he buried his head in heaving sobs, "You can repay me by going next door and telling the man who looks just like me what you have told me." The stranger did and now both brothers were weeping for their foolishness. They realized the distance that they had fostered, the walls they had built, the years that they had wasted, the selfish pride. It all happened for no reason at all. And they also realized that it took an unexpected third presence, call him the Reconciler, to make it clear and right again.

~

Life happens like that – not always so clean and clear – but honestly, it does. You know it and so do I. Walls go up and distance builds and misunderstandings get larger than life and so often for the most senseless of reasons. The story so sadly illustrates what a spirit of mistrust can do to a relationship. And it can happen just like that to individuals, families, congregations, communities, even between nations.

But in the face of that we are given our Biblical truth and it is an awesome one to behold. God intervenes, quite often in the face of the unexpected. God reconciles, most ironically where we are most deeply stuck. God breaks the chain of confusion, most surely when we think there is no other way.

That's what Paul was saying in the first century and his words are so promising. "God was in Christ reconciling the world to himself, not counting their trespasses against them, but entrusting this reconciliation to them." More: "If anyone is in Christ there is a new creation! The old has passed away! Everything has become new!"

This is pure mystery, pure grace, pure gift! And this is the promise. That, as for Paul, when we really take hold of this truth, a transformational moment descends, a seismic shift, a sea change at the core of who we are. Because once we have received that gift, once we have let the change into our hearts, once we have become reconciled, nothing can really be the same again. It is infectious. We become reconcilers to others, too. We become bearers of making things right. We become, as Paul calls, Ambassadors for Christ.

I suspect that in lots of ways those two brothers are something of an archetype. They each live in us in the brokenness of the world. But the truth transcends from beyond as the Reconciler, the Human Face of God, has the power to set us free from all manner of stuckness, and who then invites and empowers us to follow.

> *"You shall be called the repairer of the breach."*
> *Isaiah 58: 12*

Chapter Five: Celebrations and Seasons

Christian Faith lives between two great mysteries.

*The first is the mystery of the incarnation and the
amazing story of a God who would come close enough to have skin on.
It is hard for most of us to fathom the depths of what this is about:
that God so loved the world as to choose to come dwell
amid the likes of human beings.*

*The second is the mystery of the resurrection which tells us that God's
presence and promise are on this side of life and far beyond;
that even the hardest of hearts could not stop the living spirit of Jesus
from emerging again and again; and that in him the love of power
is overcome by the power of love.*

Geordie Campbell

~

A Moth Christmas

Every now and again I listen to National Public Radio's Moth Radio Hour. Quite simply, it's a story-telling venue that provides opportunities for people to try their hand at spinning tales of impressive variety before living audiences.

It features poignant, personal, sometimes hilarious, but mostly amazing heartfelt stories. The one qualifier is that the story must be real and belong to the teller. George Dawes Green is the brainchild of this, and he has touched a nerve of enormity as people gather in all manner of cozy theaters to listen as others tell.[51]

Essentially, he wanted to recreate the feeling of summer evenings as a child when he and his friends would gather on his back porch to hone their narrative skills. As such evenings would have it, moths were often attracted to the single light on the porch just as people were, hence the moniker Moth Radio.[52]

~

Of course, stories have their origins in all kinds of places and ways. For example, it can start with a voice at the other end of the phone line. It happened just exactly so for me.

"Mr. Campbell, I am working on a story for next Sunday's front page, and I would appreciate a few moments of your time." I have learned to be cautious about such interviews. But the season of good will prevailed and I consented.

"I'm doing a piece on celebrating Christmas. Can you tell me how you keep the Spirit of Christmas alive for your congregation?" Before I could answer she changed the question and pushed on to ask for more, "I mean how do you deal with all of the commercialism down at the church?"

"I'm not so sure what you are asking about," I said, "we don't have a lot of commercialism down at the church." Her sustained silence told me that my humor passed by her completely.

I went on. After all, I did not want to show up on the front page

---

[51] Meg Bowles, et al. How To Tell a Story: The Essential Guide to Memorable Storytelling from the Moth. Crown Publishing, 2022.
[52] Google: NPR Moth, Wikipedia, 2019.

of a major newspaper as a pastoral pest! So, I reframed what I heard beneath her question: "Perhaps you are wondering how we keep the spiritual dimension of the season at the center in the midst of a culture steeped in materialism?"

"Yes, exactly, that's what I meant. So how do you do that at your church?" I picked it up, "Well, Christmas is about the mystery of Jesus being born into the world, and what it means to have God's presence right here on earth."

"So, we tell stories and sing about his coming and birth in a variety of ways. We remember him and celebrate our belief in the good news that God comes to us in unique and unpredictable moments, as unexpected as a baby born in some hay."

"We do that with music and scripture, programs and pageants. We bring together the values of justice and joy, mercy and love, that Jesus taught the world. We believe he is the best model we have of how God wants us to live."

I felt like I was making an important affirmation about my own faith. You can understand then, why her follow-up question made my head spin wildly. "Well, what about the Christmas tree? Isn't that just as much the center of it all?"

The teacher in me explained that the Christmas tree, while a tradition that I treasure, is not directly related to the birth of the child in the manger at all. I even dared the ground of telling her that Christmas trees were pagan.

That didn't stop her. In fact, I think it may have offended her. "Well, if Christmas trees aren't a spiritual symbol what would be an appropriate Christian symbol of the holiday?" I could feel the slippery slope on which I was standing getting steeper.

"The creche is the most important one to me," I said. I told her about remembering the story through narrative, that we have two accounts of what happened in Bethlehem, and a third one that is more like poetry, and that a creche helps me to imagine the strands of stories that we have.

My heart sunk completely when she responded almost deadpan, "what's a creche?" My eyes rolled in disbelief, undetectable to her, and I honestly found myself hoping that she would abandon her article in favor of something she was more qualified to write about.

The interview went on a little while beyond that, but I'll stop here. And in all fairness, I have to say that she did frame my thoughts reasonably well in a holiday feature that blended my words with the comments of a few other colleagues.[53]

~

But I think I let it end too soon. I wish I had also said more. I wish I had said something like this. Believing in Jesus, being a Christian, is not a moment that happened only once in history. It wasn't a one-off event. It's present, and ongoing, and keeps unfolding. I'd tell her that it's a process of mystery and transformation that commands an entire shift in human identity. And then I'd try to entice her with this story.[54]

---

[53] Bonnie G. Dresner. "Remembering the Meaning of Christmas" in The Hartford Courant, December 17, 1995, p. 1.
[54] Chandler W. Gilbert. When I Open My Window. Grenfell Reading Center, 2001, pp. 44-45.

There was once a retreat in a spacious lodge on top of a mountain in the Poconos. It was the week after Christmas. As the event was ending one of the leaders gave the final blessing. He asked them to face outward through the wide bank of tall windows that displayed the hills and valleys of earth spread out before them.

He had them repeat with him a beautiful verse from scripture: "God has made of one blood all of the nations of the earth."

Then he asked them to raise their hands in a benediction over the whole world. He reminded them that their first names were given to them when they were born – names like Jim and Susan, Wendy and Scott.

But their last name, he said, is the name given by virtue of their faith. That name is Christ. And then he told them that they are called to "be Christs" to each other, to the nation, and to the whole of planet earth.

~

Now, to any who are listening on Moth Radio Hour . . . *that's* how to keep the spirit of Christmas alive. Be as Christ to one another!

Mistakes Preachers Make

Here's a secret about church life that most people already know. Every single congregation worth of the name has its own handful of unforgettable characters. Really, it is so. Sometimes such memorable creatures are only a few in number and other times they are quite generously populated.

Among my collection of such folks, over a field of four churches, was a man by the name of Gene Godt. He was a key player in my first parish in Vermont. A sweeter, kinder guy you could not find anywhere in the world. He was old-school polite, smart, funny, curious, and soft as a pussycat. Notably, he loved to charm the ladies, most especially the pastor's wife!

And Gene was, how should I say it? Loquacious! He loved to talk and could do so about anything, with considerable intelligence, and for a long time. That gift for gab often placed him in conversations in which he was not shy in offering his opinions, and at times creating a ruckus.

That's why I knew that I was in for it when Gene came at me briskly and face-straight after the first Christmas Sunday I led in the Newfane Congregational Church. He, being retired from a distinguished career in broadcasting, considered his wisdom would be quite useful to me as a green-behind-the-ears public speaker, so he did not hold back.

"Young man," he chimed, "you preachers all make the same mistake." He intentionally spoke loudly enough such that others heard him and turned their ears our way. "I'm telling you this because I like you and I want you to succeed in your ministry. You'll go far someday. I want you to always remember that it started with this advice."

I was trying to appear calm, but my mind raced at warp-speed. Did I say something unorthodox or even stupid? Did I mispronounce an important word? Did I ignore making eye contact with him? Worst of all: did I lose the congregation entirely as I waxed eloquent with my well-schooled interpretation of the Bethlehem mystery?

"Actually," he corrected himself, "not just one mistake. You preachers all make two mistakes with remarkably consistency. It is honestly, quite annoying."

"The first is that you use big words when simple ones would do much better. Words like incarnation, cherubim, numinous, ineffable, omniscient, and inexplicable are not very helpful to any of us. Who talks like that anyway? And making statements like 'he was in the beginning with God, all things were made through him and without him was not anything made that was made.' Ye gads! Give me a break!"

"The second thing is much larger and more important. Listen very carefully now. I want you to pay attention. Don't brush this off. You don't let us sing enough Christmas carols. We wait all year, get barely a week's worth of singing in, and then boom, we're done. It's all over. You shut us down."

"You might find it instructive to know that the last three preachers I spoke to about this aren't here any longer! I've heard all the babble you preachers have about theological integrity and purity or some such arguments."

"Don't they teach you in those seminary schools that singing the carols we love and hearing the stories is sometimes the best way, maybe the only way, to speak about the things that matter most? Mark my words! You can never go wrong with stories and songs."

I was seriously trying to collect my wits at this point. He could see that, and to ease the moment he broke into his classic laugh and winked in his Gene-only-knew-how-to-do-it-way. And then he said Merry Christmas and wrapped me in a hug as he also wiped tears from his cheeks.

As we parted, he said, "By the way, young man. You are most welcome for my wise advice. You'll remember this moment years from now. Go lighter on the words that no one knows or wants to know; and let us sing the songs that we long for."

With genuine thanks to ole' Gene, I have never swayed from his wise advice.

> *"And in that region, there were shepherds in the field*
> *keep watch over their flock by night."*
> *Luke 2:8*

Gentle Revolutionary

Did you know that the earliest Christmas carol predates the first Christmas? The best of scholarly agreement places it six months before the Bethlehem birth. It has been variously named over time: the *Song of Mary*, the *Canticle of Mary*, the *Carol of Mary,* and in the Byzantine tradition the *Ode of the Theotokos*. Most of us recognize it by a more classical name, the *Magnificat*.[55]

The Magnificat is one of the eight most ancient Christian hymns that we can identify. As such, it has earned Mary the credit for being the first Christian disciple; for even after only three months of carrying her child, she was becoming the spokesperson of the ideals and values that his all-too-brief life would give to the world.[56]

~

She begins her carol in rejoicing. Eugene Peterson translates her first words, "I am bursting with Good News; I am dancing the song of my God!" Or, more traditionally: "My soul magnifies the Lord, and my Spirit rejoices in God my Savior!"

Either way, I love that the word and spirit of rejoicing are in there somewhere. It's not a benign statement. It's an expansive premonition. There was a largeness growing in her not only because she was with child. At the same time God was doing something to make her soul larger to bear all that was to come, most of which she had no way of knowing yet. And the practice of rejoicing, of breathing gladness, is one way to stretch our hearts toward this amazing gift of God.

---

[55] Google "Magnificat" for some fascinating history.
[56] Raymond E. Brown. <u>The Coming of Christ in Advent</u>. The Liturgical Press, 1988, pp. 60-71.

Martin Copenhaver correctly notes that rejoicing is key to celebrating the birth of Christ. He says that we need practice it because it's not always or even often a natural thing to do. In fact, for some of us it is not ever at all easy. His words: "We need to practice rejoicing not because this is a particularly bright time, but precisely so because it is dark; and yet, even here, in the darkness, the light of the world is coming."[57]

So, Mary names it, claims it, sings it: "My soul magnifies the Lord! My heart rejoices! I am bursting with good news!"

~

And then her expanding soul reaches deeper. She sings about the value of life with poetic phrases and words. There is a topsy-turvy switch-out she is experiencing and expressing. "God has looked with favor on the least and the lowly." In true humility she described herself as "in my lowly estate." But then she sings of being lifted-up, reidentified, named, and known as more than she had ever learned to see in herself before.

I wonder. Can you see the progression? Rejoicing enlarges the soul and leads to a revaluing in life, something that begins with a deep awareness of being loved by God, which extends to all people, and to all the world.

~

And then she adds the unexpected: revolution! We may remember Mary as gentle and tender which is true, but she was also revolutionary. The vision of a better world apprehended and propelled her in profound ways.

---

[57] Martin Copenhaver, "Rejoice!" in Hark! Advent Devotionals. UCC Still Speaking Authors, 2012, p. 16.

Dietrich Bonhoeffer once wrote, "Mary's song does not have sweet nostalgic or even playful tones. It is, instead, a hard, strong, inexorable claim about collapsing the thrones and lords of this world; it's about the power of God and the powerlessness of humankind."[58]

A colleague of mine has a curious way of greeting his congregation on Christmas Eve. He says, "Merry Christmas and welcome. If you came tonight expecting a tame story, you came to the wrong place. If you came for a story that does not threaten you in some way, you came for a different story than the one we tell. But if you came for a story of reversals; if you came to be reminded that God loves you too much to leave you unchanged; if you came to follow the light, even if it blinds you; if you came for salvation and not safety, then, ah, my friends, you are in precisely the right place."[59]

And then he asks with a pause that surveys the room: "So, what are you here for?"

~

What an amazing Christmas Carol Mary sang before Jesus was even born! Rejoicing her way to a larger soul; revaluing life as God intends for every breathing, living being; and inciting a spirit of revolution until the world is whole and peaceful and loving and fair.

I don't know the melody she sang, but I so love her words! I hope that you will hold them in heart with me as Christmas comes again.

'He has brought down the powerful from their thrones and

---

[58] Dietrich Bonhoeffer. The Mystery of Holy Night. Crossroad Books, 1996, p. 6.
[59] Quinn Caldwell. All I Really Want. Abingdon Press, 2012, pp. 110-112.

*lifted up the lowly; he has filled the hungry with good things
and sent the rich away empty.
Luke 1: 52-53*

Unto Whom?

I am delighted to be with you this morning, this being my last of fifteen Christmas Sundays as your pastor.[60] My heart overflows with all the gladness that it can hold. Though, I'll admit, too, some sadness is in there as well. Bittersweet is a word that fits.

But even in the glad and sad blend unique to me this time around, we have the Christmas story to keep us on track. Even more, we are each meant to get all tangled up in it!

Today is not a spectator's moment but one of invitation. We are a part of this holy birthing, participants in the transforming, purveyors of these inexplicable things that once upon a long-ago time came to pass.

~

I hope we might discover this and find it exactly so, at least in part, as we listen to the angel Gabriel from Bethlehem's sky. "I bring you good news that will come to *all the people*."

Note that phrase: *all the people*. That feels so good and wholesome and right to me. Especially at a time when we are so encamped and hunkered down, so polarized and divided, so politicized, so surrounded by walls to keep us in and walls to keep others out.

But here it is, straight from the heart of an angel who speaks for God: this Christmas gift of light and life and hope is for *all the people*. The only credential we need to receive it is to be fully human as God created us to be.

---

[60] Preached on Christmas Sunday, 2019. This was my last Christmas as Senior Pastor of First Church Congregational, UCC in West Hartford CT, one month shy of my retirement in January 2020.

Gabriel said it like that to poor shepherds, grungy from work, in the dark of night, and in fields abiding. This amazing gift, this incarnate, mysterious, life-giving, grace-holding presence of God that comes to earth for everyone and crawls in beside us. Poor and rich, north and south, east and west, starved and stuffed, settled or wandering.

And we don't have to look an inch beyond that story to see this ripple. There are business folks tending an Inn; shepherds, close to the earth and lowly; Herod in his addiction to power and royalty and entitlement; Magi seeking truth from afar. We have angels on high and animals on low. And most unexpectedly present: a simple carpenter's family with child.

Surely, this must mean that this God of ours has a heart so large that we cannot even begin to fathom any boundaries or lines of distinction because they are simply not there. Christmas shouts this out across the centuries in creeds and carols to colors and cultures so far beyond our comprehension that we can't even begin to imagine or count.

~

But then there is more from Bethlehem's sky: unto all people, yes, but also *unto you*.

That brings it galaxies closer and about as personal as could ever be. God, present, in this time, here and now, in the flesh of life. A God with skin on. Not just in biblical memory or ancient abstractions, but on this wounded and beautiful earth, in this land, in our town, in this sacred room, in your very life. The dwelling, beating, loving, reaching heart of God is right here.

He asked that I call him Robert as we first met. He was the keynote presenter at a writer's conference I attended some time ago in North Carolina.[61] He's an author, a mystic, a spiritual person of renown. He is also a soul whose depth of wisdom about the human condition came to him through the unlikely teacher of serious clinical depression.

He told us about it by recalling a Christmas Eve somewhere in his forties. "I went to the Christmas Candlelight Service tonight, desperately mining for something of light to help me make my way. I heard the story of Jesus' birth, again. I sang the carols that I know by heart, again. I held a candle, again."

"As I drove home, a line in one of the songs would not stop in me: 'Let every heart prepare him room.' Suddenly, like a flash of holy light I realized just then what I needed most of all. It was to hope against my own hopelessness that the child of whom I was singing would actually be born in me and grow."

Everything changed with that realization. Call it a moment of conversion, or a leap of faith, or a sudden insight. Or call it Christmas alive. *Unto you and unto all people* and it is just exactly so!

~

Let me invite a pocketful of others to ride on Gabriel's coattails. Because the truth that Gabriel spoke from that nighttime sky belongs to all of us, individually and collectively, in some pretty life changing ways, if we could only hear it.

---

[61] Robert Benson. <u>Between the Dreaming and the Coming True</u>. Harper/Collins, 1996, pp. 106-108.

Saint Augustine: "This birth is always happening. But if it does not happen in me, what good shall ever come? What matters most is my choice that the birth shall happen in me."

Thomas Merton: "Christ is born. He is born to us. And he is born today. For Christmas is not merely another day in the weary round of time. It is a day when eternity enters time, and time is caught up into eternity."

Martin Luther: "Notice how Gabriel does not simply say, Christ is born, but to you he is born. Neither does he say, I bring glad tidings, but to you I bring glad tidings of great joy. This joy was not only to remain in Christ, but it shall be to all the people. It enables all who believe it to receive life as their own. This is simply the way the Gospel operates."

Frederick Buechner: "What keeps the wild hope of Christmas alive year after year in a world notorious for dashing all hopes is the haunting dream that the child who was born that day may yet be born again, even in us and to us."

~

And so, my dear Christmas friends.

However you might discover this birth awaiting in your life – for *unto you* is born a savior and *unto me*.

Wherever you might find his amazing gift of grace with and among the company and community of others - for *unto all of us* he is born.

Whenever you see the signs of peace and reconciliation pop-up in the unexpected mix of human life, of justice and joy and compassion and kindness - *unto earth and all her people* he is born.

Now you tell me. What closer, better, more hope-filled gift could any of us or the whole world ever need to have and to hold? May it be ever so.

> *"I bring you good news of great joy for all people.*
> *For unto you is born this day a savior who is Christ the Lord.*
> *Luke 2:10 - 11*

Be Not Afraid

The mystery of Christmas Eve[62] settles down in and around us now. And, as Marcellus said in Hamlet, "so hallowed and gracious is the time."[63] It is, indeed, both of these.

By now most of the tasks of preparing and wrapping are at rest or nearly so. At least I hope they are. We come to Church, a perfect time for a sacred pause if ever there was one, a time to catch our spiritual breath. Carols lift and sooth even in the raw places of life. Candles flicker away the darkness. Most of all, the Bethlehem story brings to focus the things that matter most. And then, we come to the Table as the Christ Child becomes for us the Bread of Life. At its very best that's what Christmas Eve delivers: holiness beyond speaking, and a grace that descends all around the earth.

Marcellus got it just right: hallowed and gracious. And then Horatio answered. His response was a bit more in the shadows and conveyed a tentative affirmation mixed-up with his own hesitation: "So I have heard and do *in part* believe."

To be fair, Horatio was simply caught in his own honest way, stuck in-between grace and grit no doubt, both told and heard. And his ever-so-human response belongs to all the human family: "So we have heard and do *in part* believe."

I wonder: have you have felt the edges of Horatio's hesitation? That even with the hallowed and gracious time that Marcellus has so

---

[62] Preached on Christmas Eve, 2019. This was my last Christmas Eve Service as Senior Pastor of First Church Congregational, UCC in West Hartford CT, one month shy of my retirement in January 2020.
[63] Frederick Buechner. The Faces of Jesus. Paraclete Press, 1974, p. 14.

aptly named, there's that catch, a cloud, a condition, something unsettled that suspends the full capacity of our own yes?

Lord knows, there are lots of reasons to believe only part way. Life's ambiguities create all sorts of dissonance for us. Our enlightened minds want more to go on; the never-ending dilemmas and tangles of human life press in; and worries small and not-so-small distract us with amazing consistency.

These present days it seems that the most prevalent distraction that gets in the way is fear. Not just individually but collectively as well. And as these tumultuous times reveal to us, people who are afraid can be led in some God-awful ways, and say some horrible things, and distort this God-so-loved-world into so much less.

But it goes way back to the beginning. Because the primary distraction for the shepherds on that first Christmas was fear as well. In the King's English, "they were sore afraid." But afraid of what? Of an angel? Or maybe of the dark, literal or metaphoric. Or perhaps of the very uncertain times in which they wandered with their sheep? Fear of what the world was coming to? Or even this: fear of what might come to the world if they fell for the story and followed the Christ Child?

So, let's take a healing breath together. We have this wisdom as an antidote. The long witness of Christian faith tells us that the manger is where hope enters the world and contends with fear. The angel told the shepherds straight up: be not afraid!

Did you know that phrase is used more in the Bible than any other? In fact, depending on whom you read, it appears as many as three hundred and sixty-five times! How perfectly convenient!

Three hundred sixty-five! So, should we avail ourselves of this Good News, we have the encouragement every day to live with hope rather than in fear! What a gift!

Parker Palmer writes, "We have places of fear inside us, but we have other places as well: places with names like trust and hope and faith." And we need to name them and claim them, especially now, giving them and living them. That's what Christmas invites. And it is what the world sorely needs.

These are tumultuous days, indeed. But for tonight, so perfectly noted by Marcellus, "so hallowed and gracious is the time," may we let go of the fears that are so rampant just now and take hold of the hope.

And, without apology or judgement, may we surrender the archetypal hesitation of Horatio and tweak his words ever so slightly: "So we have heard . . . and do *in full* believe."

How silently, how silently, the wondrous gift is given. O come let us adore him! Together. Right here. Right now.

"Mary treasured all these things and pondered them in her heart."
Luke 2:19

A Dawning Thing

*Easter is a dawning thing
whose truth requires time
to sink in and take hold.*

*It's a mysterious thing,
not of the natural order,
breaking all prior assumptions -*

*causing the human mind
to run in larger and larger circles.
It's a dissonant thing*

*where the distance
between the expected
and the realized*

*turns completely upside down.
Could it really be? But how?
This makes no sense at all.*

*Those who got to the tomb
at first light were perplexed
and confused, fearful and running.*

*But then, to give it time to settle,
as leaven in the loaf,
a transformation rises from within.*

*It's a dawning thing alright,
slow and silent in revealing,
as God's new horizon awakens.*

Warm Easter Fuzzies

Sometimes I just like a good story that brings me a smile. Life can get such that I don't do that enough. Smile that is. It's not that I don't feel it. It's just that I keep it in.

So, here are two Easter stories that bring my smile out. Interpret them as you might, but to me they are simply feel good warm fuzzies that sprinkle the lighter side of promise all over my day.

By the way, just so you know, preachers are known for being collectors of such things. We are always on the hunt for a story that will tell well and will bring a smile to the waiting face of others. Especially on a day like Easter. These two are of that sort. In both cases, the author is unknown.

~

Winston Churchill, a very large name in history's storehouse, planned his own funeral. It took place at St. Paul's Cathedral. Pam and I had the privilege of visiting that site when we were traveling in London.

It's an awesome building with a high and magnificent dome that dwarfs the nave below. And there were two things that Churchill very specifically requested with that dome in mind.

After the benediction, silence would fall over the gathered crowd. Then a bugler high in the dome would play the familiar sound of "taps." These notes were to bring home the realization that a life had come to an end.

"However," instructed Churchill, "once taps have sounded, and after a pause, another bugler will begin to play from across the expanse of the dome. These will be the notes of 'reveille.'"

He wanted this because he believed that mortal things are never the last things; our small human lifespan is but part of the landscape of God's larger holding, and the final sounds of history will not be "taps" but "reveille."

~

"There is a story about a woman who was near to her death and wanted to plan her funeral. She called for her pastor. He accommodated her immediately with a visit later that day.

They talked together with tenderness and candor about all the details. She decided on the scriptures that would be read and the hymns that would be sung. "Nothing schmaltzy," she commanded. "And no funeral dirges. Just sweet loving songs of Jesus."

And then she said to him, "When I die, I want to be laid out in my best dress. And I want you to send me off with my Bible in my left hand." The minister nodded and acknowledged her well-worn Bible on the nightstand.

She went on, "And I want a fork in my right hand." Now he was confused. All the details so far had been all right, but a fork made no sense. She was quick to explain, "You know I love church. And one of the things that I've loved the most are the potluck suppers. I've been to a million of them! And at the best of those suppers, when it was just about over someone would come to take away my plate and they'd whisper, 'keep your fork.' That always told me that there was a great dessert coming – not just Jell-O or junket or brownies, but chocolate cake or homemade pie. So, when they said, 'keep your fork,' I knew the best was yet to come."

~

May your smile bring a Warm Fuzzy Easter to someone who needs a light touch of promise!

The Locked Room

"Spontaneous remission is what we call such things." Dr. Nurko's eyes blinked with astonishment as he squinted through tears. His manner and glance were full of empathy and grace as he smiled at Annabel and her mother.

He's a specialist at Children's Hospital in Boston, a man of significant renowned for his expertise in pediatric digestive diseases for obstructive motility disorder. Annabel and her mother Christie became his patients as they searched the vast medical world for someone, _anyone_, who could help them.

They came all the way from Texas, their circumstances filled with despair and illness, healing and hope. It's a true story with dead ends and open doors; with faith lost and regained; with all the twists and turns of a young family and their ride through the maze of medical care; with months of airplanes and medication, hospitalizations and disappointment, and with the eventual advice from Dr. Nurko to Christie, "Best to spend as much quality time with her as you can."

Until. Until by various chain of circumstance, or maybe providence, Annabel climbed a cottonwood tree back home in their side-yard at the daring of her sister. It was hollowed and rotted. A branch broke and she fell into the tree plunging headfirst. Miraculously, the impact to her head jarred something in her brain and the disease disappeared. Or was it, perhaps, those suspended minutes between life and death when an encounter with God told her that she would be healed?

"Spontaneous remission," the doctor said. "Miracles from Heaven" is what the movie is called. It's a powerful Easter story of hope out of despair and life out of near-death. And it's true, no matter how you might choose to interpret the truth.

~

That story opens the way to another story, this one of biblical renown. It, too, is full of truth in any and every way you might ever interpret such things. It's filled with wounds and fear, astonishment and disbelief, locked doors and unexpected outcomes. But mostly it's about Easter and hope, presence and power and life.

Let's travel back as we listen. It's early evening on the first Easter, this according to the gospel of John. The disciples were still soaked in the sadness of recent days but also quickened and bewildered by something that Mary Magdalene had said, "I have seen the Master!" This was corroborated by two of the disciples, at least in part. So now the whole bunch of them were overcome by amazement, yes, but also in abject fear that the religious authorities who had done Jesus in would come after them next. And so, they locked all the doors in the house, and especially the door to the room they were in.

And then somehow, through walls that were solid and doors that were locked tight, Jesus entered and stood among them. Wait! How in the world? Huh? This is not possible! Dumbfounded. Dazed. Speechless.

And then, as if that wasn't enough, he showed them the wounds in his hands and side - apparently to dissuade any wondering that he might be an apparition of some sort. Then he spoke in the voice that always calmed them deep down: "Peace to you," not only once but twice just to be sure.

~

So do the obvious wondering with me! How did he ever get in? Either the locked doors, remember there was more than one of them, were not real, or the Risen Christ was *more* real than material boundaries. Either the solid walls were not real, or Jesus was *more* real than the walls. Either their fears were not real, or he was *more* real than anything that they knew or expected or could fully believe.

~

Some stories from the Bible are called "thick stories." This is clearly one of them. Thick stories are layered. They are not singular. They provide different clues of detail and contact and connection. They are suggestive and hint and hunch and point – all to keep the human mind wondering.

And this story about fear and insecurity; about locks and walls and barriers; about tangible signs like wounds and calming sounds like voices; about the want for evidence-based believing which, then and now, is thick as thick can ever be.

~

Even more: this story is important enough that John reports it happened a second time. Eight days later, the same thing, the same room, the same locked doors, the same solid walls, the same Jesus. The same wounds: still raw, palpable, touchable, and undeniable. The same words and the same resonant promise, "peace be with you." And the same breath of life from the one who had died.

Do the wondering again. Either his death was not real, or the breath of his life is *more* real than dying. Either he wasn't there, and they were all hallucinating, or his presence was *more* real than all boundaries and separation, *more* real than all measures of time and space, and of heaven and earth.

Now, if the stalwart doubled-guarded doors of fear can't keep out God's grace from showing up; or the confusion and uncertain moments of life that come to bear can't keep us away from God's love or healing or hope what can? Paul was to write of this in times to come, "Nothing, but nothing, but nothing . . . can separate us from the love of God."

John ends his story with one more promise. He tells us, in essence, this is not the end of things to come, only the beginning. Because, in his words, "Jesus provides far more God-revealing signs than can be written down in one book."

~

Whether by Annabel's spontaneous remission and countless stories of real life-giving faith in the hearts of real people; or by the story of disciples living in fear and hiding behind locked doors . . . the power of resurrection and Easter and hope and life and healing are all around us, all the time. Even those little hunches, or maybe especially those, for which we have no way to express or words to speak, except for the poet[64] . . .

A thousand thousand small deaths
blows to my spirit
wounds to my soul
hurts to my body
entanglements of mind
humanity reduced, nearly destroyed.

---

[64] Ruth Burgess and Kathy Galloway, eds. Praying for the Dawn. Wild Goose Publications, 2000, p. 170.

A thousand thousand tiny resurrections
my spirit uplifted
my soul rested
my body healing
my mind refreshed, enlightened
humanity restored, reaching for hope.

A new life?
Redeemed?
I don't know.
The specifics of the Christian faith pass me by.
But I think, perhaps I'm learning
something of death and resurrection.

~

I think, perhaps, I am learning, too.

Something of the mystery that floats in the thin space between heaven and earth; something of locked doors but open hearts; something of hope and healing; something of death and resurrection.

Happy Easter! In the Living Spirit of Jesus!

Henry's Last and First Breath

On the night that Pam's grandfather died I was caught up in a dream. Henry, as I was fond of calling him, had been suffering with cancer and was in a nursing home in Pennsylvania. It had been a very difficult time.

In the dream I was in Henry's room and he was agitating and crying. Blinding and bright sun was shining through the window and bothering his eyes terribly. He wanted me to pull down the shade and turn out the light. But no matter what I tried to do, I could not comfort him.

I woke up in a cold sweat.

A little while later I drifted off to sleep and had almost the exact same dream again, the same sequence, the same helplessness, the same cold sweat.

A third time I fell asleep. The same sequence followed, except this time when it got to the most helpless and frustrating part of the dream, I left Henry's room and went out and stood in a meadow. I was watching the sun in the evening sky. It was full of peace and an eternal promise of glory.

Suddenly, I looked to my side and Henry was standing right beside me. This was quite odd because it was the first time he had walked in months. His cane, walker and wheelchair were no longer necessary.

He assured me that it was okay. That all would be well. That the moment had come. That it was time to go home. Henry and I watched the sun set together. It was nothing less than beautiful, nothing shy of perfect. There was nothing to fear. He was completely free.

Moments later Pam and I were awakened by a phone call in our Boston apartment, 500 miles away. It was Pam's mother calling to tell us that Henry had just died.

You see it's bigger, this mystery that we live. It's about birth and about death, about love and grace, about hope and promise. And it's beyond the veil. All of it is beyond the veil. And God is always so much larger, on this side and the other. So much more than we know, and galaxies beyond.

Easter Arise!

Awesome God of Easter Promise
You have taken the world by surprise all over again!
You have transformed and redeemed
the impossibilities of life
and cleared a new way!

You have opened us with joy to
mystery and power, presence and mercy and hope!
Most astonishing you have done
all of this in love and with grace,
free for the taking!

We pray now that the fullness of
the blessing of the Risen Christ would surround us.
That where life is in despair
or hearts are burdened,
your dawn and light might begin to rise.

That where there seems
to be no way at all, you will make ways for new life to emerge.
And most especially, where there is conflict,
or the threat of war;
where there is division and strife and fear,

you will move in and through our time and lives
to bring the world to reconciliation,
harmony, justice, and peace.
O God, we beseech you: let our beating Easter hearts rise!
Amen!

Chapter 6: The Other Side

*"Yesterday a child came out to wander,
caught a dragonfly inside a jar,
fearful when the sky was full of thunder,
and tearful at the falling of a star.*

*And the seasons, they go round and round,
and the painted ponies go up and down.
We're captive on the carousel of time.
we can't return, we can only look,
behind from where we came,
and go round and round and round,
in the circle game."*

Joni Mitchell

~

What Time Is It?

I knew a guy in seminary with an uncanny ability to tell time without ever glancing toward a clock. He didn't wear a watch either, in fact, I'm not quite sure that he even owned one. And yet, he was spot-on accurate nearly 100% of the time.

We all know that people are gifted in different ways, and for him, an awareness of time was just an intuitive kind of thing. It was a felt-sense, bone-deep, inner sort of knowing he had come to trust, and a capacity that he could neither fully understand nor explain.

Now and again, and all in fun, we'd test him: "Hey Tom, what time is it?" He would respond instantly: "seven after three." If any of us corrected him saying something like, "You're four minutes ahead, it's only three after three" he would trump us up one, "No, you are four minutes behind." And then he would sweeten the fun with advice, "You need to get your watches checked!"

He was so consistently correct that some of us began to refer to him affectionately as "Greenwich Mean" not because he was mean, but because he became our standard bearer. Other times we called him "Big Ben."

~

But Tom was his real name, and he was a master at what the early Greek thinkers called *chronos*. Chronos is the kind of time that we can measure and mark and to which we apply other terms like late, early, soon, linear, sequential, and quantitative.

It's the tick-tock granular kind of time we track in seconds, minutes, and hours, and eventually days and weeks, months and years. It's where chronicles are begun and chronologies form; and where we impose other devices like calendars, hourglasses, sundials, schedules, and deadlines.

The Greek philosophers were also aware of another dimension of time as well. This is the kind of time called <u>*kairos*</u>. Rather than the more granular chronos, kairos is more like time at 30,000 feet. It refers not to the sequence of time, but much deeper, to a having a sensitivity and consciousness for the right moment for a certain thought or action.

Kairos is more spiritual; more numinous; more suggestive of the deeper dimension of eternity and purpose. It is not measurable. It is ontological. It has a qualitative character that asks not "what time is it?" but "what is this moment in my life and what does it mean?"

Madeline L'Engle once wrote about rocking her granddaughter to sleep. As she took the child and sat down, she was distracted by the pure tick-tock of chronos and the monkey-mind-chatter of tasks and appointments as we all carry in our minds. But the moment turned to kairos as she sank into the eternal delight of cuddling her sweet one to the kind of rest that only babies seem to remember how to do.[65]

So, we have chronos represented by tick-tock and alarm clocks; and kairos as we find the deep moments of life beyond any measure of time.

~

Hold these two dimensions of time as I introduce you to another friend. This one is a literary companion of mine and of the ages. He is known as Qoheleth, a name synonymous with Quester, Questioner, Gatherer and Teacher. History also remembers him as Ecclesiastes.

Ecclesiastes asked, in both poetry and prose, about where we are in our own life and along our own journey. He was far deeper in his wondering about time. And he did so by holding up the oscillations that all of us come to experience in the passing of our years.

"To everything there is a season," he wrote, "and a time for every purpose under heaven." He went on to juxtapose 28 contrasting moments along life's way. He named them for us on the upside,

---

[65] Madeline L'Engle. <u>The Crosswicks Journal: A Circle of Quiet</u>. Harper Books, 1972, pp. 244-45.

which I suspect we most prefer to ponder: birth and healing, laughing and dancing and loving and peace. But also more shadowed: dying and weeping, mourning and casting away, war and hate.

Qoheleth was trying to sort and make sense of this mystery of time in all its shadows and light, in all its circles and cycles and turnings and stops and starts. And ultimately, he affirmed what we most need to know. That time is a sacred mystery offered and held under the eternal purview and providence of God.

~

So, take these thoughts and wonder: What time might it be for you, and what time for me?

The clock time, the *chronos* time is easy and quantifiable as my friend Tom could tell so amazingly well. It's the time we number and tell.

But what of the deeper call of your life's time? What of the *kairos*, the gift we measure not in minutes but in moments? Are you living as you would want to be? Am I?

Even more: are we spending this irreplaceable gift of our lives in pleasing ways for God?

"For everything there is a season,
and a time for every matter under heaven."
Ecclesiastes 3: 1

Nostalgia

Summer breezes were always fair
and kites rarely crashed as they tugged
their string from the sky.
Do you remember?

Hills were never too steep
that a good climb could not overcome
and the view on top was forever.
Wasn't it just so?

Friendships were for playing
and nothing seemed more complex
than waiting in line for the swing.
Can you recall?

Nostalgia is a mighty force,
a prism that stretches and bends the edges
to better and more than once was.
Or does it, really?

Do you remember?
Wasn't it just so?
Am I getting this right?
Or is it all a figment of my imagining?

Vapor Trails

*Half a dozen in one glance
placing white lines on a pallet of blue sky -
vapor trails in close parallel, some crisscrossing others
as they form in the tailwind of planes
beginning their descent.*

*Someone is on the way somewhere,
leaving or landing, going far away or coming back,
departing one port for another. And in a carry-on satchel
overhead might be a baguette baked in Paris, single malt
distilled in Oban or fine woolens made by Dublin hands.*

*And this, too. A small boy waits at the gate
for his grandfather's adoring arms, or a soldier returns
to the home soil she loves; or a student arrives
for a semester abroad; or a reunion brimmed
with the taste of love's tomorrow.*

*Leaving and landing.
Coming and going. Gladness and sadness. Vapor trails
bring people together and ignite the soul's longing.
They conjure dreaming and wonder. I know such things
because, no longer young,
I am still that small boy waiting.*

A Different Way

*A long stretch of living and striving,
of pacing and racing and pushing and driving -
matter much less now and almost dissolve,
as sixty-plus offers a different resolve.*

*Life opens free, and quite unexpected,
enhancing the gift with a larger perspective,
when most of the rules of an earlier day
seem not as important, at least in this way:*

*where climbing and earning and achieving and such,
winning and contest lose their old clutch;
noise settles down and clamor much less
as questions of age rise up to bless.*

*What is the purpose of life's hard-spent years?
Where is the fruit of the joy and the tears?
And how does one conjure the fury and flatter?
When is it finished, and does it much matter?*

*"Just this," the voice of wisdom speaks forth,
"the years and the movement all have their worth;
but now is the time to settle and mentor
and to see life's horizon inviting us deeper.*

*Age speaks in ways that no one could predict,
and offers understanding and acceptance to wit.
Whatever would be if we had solely youth,
and only young growing could offer her truth?"*

The Other Side

One weekend a few years ago Pam and I traveled from New England to her hometown in Pennsylvania. Or, to put it in slightly more precise and different words, we drove nearly 800 miles to take a walk in a graveyard, the place where many of her family have found their rest.

Our visit to Lewisburg didn't bear the edges of unfinished grief and so there was not fresh sadness as we took our stroll. It was, instead, curiously, even mystically connective: something like a walk through an old neighborhood.

Pam read the names she knew and loved, now carved on gravestones. It was something like a scene from Thornton Wilder's "Our Town" bringing to awareness the presence of death in the midst of life, or maybe of the reality of life's inexorable passing toward the horizon of death.

She said somewhat wistfully, "They all live here now. They're all on the other side."

"There's Jenny," she pointed. "She always kept the neatest house, and she made really good sour-kraut."

Pam's parents and maternal grandparents were not far away from where Jenny was, just across the way as it was when they were alive.

Then a few rows down and across the lane were Uncle Bud and Aunt Dot. They were both quite influential in the community as Bud was president of the local bank. Pam had a special fondness for Aunt

Dot as her grandmother's sister, and I'm told that our daughter inherited Dot's gift for chatter and story.

The words circled back again: "They all live here now. They're all on the other side." It was rich and prime time to wonder with that phrase into deeper understanding, though neither of us had openly talked about what and where "the other side" might be.

The Bible is both clever and kind in this regard. Instead of leading us into smugness with certitude we are given metaphors, hunches, and images around which to imagine. That's as it should be. They are not meant as absolutes, rather, as holy clues to take to heart and yet also to hold very lightly.

We are given phrases like: "I shall dwell in the house of God forever." "A land flowing with milk and honey." "A new heaven and a new earth." "A banquet overflowing with hospitality." "A mansion with many rooms." "A heavenly realm which eyes have not seen, nor ears heard." And this one I just love: "In heaven a door stood open."

One of my seminary professors in seminary, Gabriel Fackre, was fond of saying that these biblical images are something like spaghetti on a cool autumn evening. You can catch the sweet aroma, the savory smell of sauce and meatballs in the kitchen, as in the next room. And though you can't see the table yet and you don't know who's coming to dinner the fragrance tells the truth: something good and rich is waiting just as promised.

Christian faith doesn't tell us too much about such images. But it proclaims in no uncertain terms that God is everywhere. Or to tangle it up in double negatives: there is nowhere that God is not, nothing that God cannot transcend, no distance that God cannot bridge.

Over time I have seen and heard voices of witness and affirmation about crossing over. I have heard it in the images and thoughts of others, the sighs and sights of those who are dying. And I have seen it in the faces and lives of families left behind in grief. The Holy Spirit, by whatever name, attends these moments.

Perhaps you have read of Eben Alexander as he journeyed into the world beyond.[66] He is the author of Proof of Heaven, an unlikely book for a clinically driven neurosurgeon to author. It enjoyed a very long ranking on the best-seller list, which tells you something of the power of his story and the hunger among us to know more. Among those pages he names and claims mystical moments wherein he was in the presence of the Divine Source of the universe itself.

In my dad's final days there were moments when it was so clear to me that he was seeing far beyond the room at the nursing home. These were not hallucinations by any stretch. They were something deeper. Something more personal. One afternoon he nearly chirped as he said "GLUM!" GLUM was what he called his grandfather, his initials being GLM, George Lincoln Moir, born on the day that Lincoln was shot. He was seeing and talking to his grandfather.

Maggie Callanan, a hospice nurse who has witnessed more than 2,000 deaths calls these "nearing death awareness" and advises caregivers and family members not to correct such claims but to allow the person to talk more about their story and experience."[67]

---

[66] Eben Alexander. MD. Proof of Heaven: A Neurosurgeon's Journey into the Afterlife. Simon and Schuster, 2012.
[67] "Crossing Over" in Century Marks, in Christian Century, July 24, 2013, p. 8.

Pam was strolling a few steps ahead of me on the southern side of the cemetery. "Over there," she nodded and gestured. "That's Larry Lawson's father. He used to own the shoe store. And over there in the next row is Mrs. Erdley. She taught at the high school with my mother."

And so, to our wondering "what's on the other side?" We have biblical images and hints, affirmations of God who transcends death, and the Holy Spirit who attends in ways we never know.

But what do you think? What *is* on the other side?

"I looked, and, oh! A Door opened into heaven.
A voice called out, "Ascend and enter and I'll show you what comes next."
Revelation 4: 1 (The Message)

Mind Fog

*Sometimes my mind feels foggy.
I search for words and find only an edge.
It's a tip of the tongue kind of thing
but deeper and more worrisome.*

*What would be left of me if I lost
the expression of language or thought
on which so much of me depends,
wordsmith that I am?*

*What if syllable and sound,
coherence and sentence dissolve between
me and another, or worse,
even me and myself?*

*It frightens me at times
when for the life of me I can't find my keys,
only to discover that they
are in my other hand.*

*And this is the shadow I fear most.
That one day I will drift to a place wherein
I won't even know that I don't
know my own name.*

The Long Goodbye

I want to tell you about a common relative of ours and the way his life came to an end.[68] His name was Moses, and he holds the honored distinction of still being the great, great grandfather of Jewish and Christian faith.

Moses was a ripe-old 120 years on his last afternoon. No matter how we interpret the Bible, that's a lot of years. Put in other words, he was a very old man.

He had just finished the considerable process of leading his people to the promised land. And of that day we are told "his eyesight was sharp; and he still walked with a spring in his step."

That's a playful way of saying that he lived at his full capacity right up to his end – body, mind, and spirit. There were no cataracts to dim his view, and he ambulated with agility and ease.

More: he had just completed a monumentally important job. It was his life's calling. Though he did not enter the promised land himself, he was able to see it from a distance. And then he died.

I suspect, in the best of all worlds, most of us would prefer our days to end like that: accomplished, healthy, clear that our work is finished, our purpose fulfilled, and held in love by those we leave behind.

~

But not all of us are afforded such gracious aging or exit. We

---

[68] Deuteronomy 34: 1-12

might grow old, at least if we are lucky enough to become elderly. But for many, our eyes do grow dim, and the spring in our step is gone.

In fact, for an increasing many, our bodies outlast our minds and intellectual capacities. The diminishment of age has its way in slow and steady measure. Measures of care become more frequent, and life becomes increasingly challenging.

Sometimes this season of diminishment and decline brings diagnostic words to the conversation that strike fear in the hearts of lots of individuals and families. The more generic term, dementia, leads the way and often is followed by the more particular diagnosis of Alzheimer's.

~

It began for Joan without her or her family's full awareness. Ever so slowly, barely noticeable changes became more evident. Forgetfulness and confusion over little things began to accumulate and gradually grew larger. Increasing bouts of anxiety and depression could be observed. Joan began to speak of others as living too long. Her family began to understand that she was speaking of her own circumstance as well.

The losses continued to compound. She would feed and search conversations for enough information to connect people and faces and places. Always very extroverted, she started to miss social events that became exhausting. Her acuity with language began to erode, and she would say "I can't think of the word. It's just off the edge of my mind."

Doctors and specialists became more present. Medications of all sorts were prescribed, numerous enough that help with taking a daily regimen of pills was retained. Agitation and frustration flared. Over the reach of several years, she fielded her shrinking world with grace and grit. But those who loved her were becoming more anguished and alarmed.

Joan gradually lost the capacity to do the things that she loved: visiting with people, reading, doing jigsaw puzzles, writing notes and cards, taking walks, talking on the phone, staying connected with old friends and with family. Even the pleasure of watching TV waned as she became convinced that the wires from the cable box would cause a fire.

Thankfully, she reached a turning point when she was more relaxed with her incapacity than her family was. In a sense, she did not know what she did not know. She adapted to the loss of much of her short-term memory and found connection more in very old memories, like her childhood and growing years. Even so, she needed increasing clues and cues from her family. Circular conversation became the mainstay of visits.

One of the very painful realities of dementia is that mixed in with significant spells of confusion there can also moments of unexpected clarity. This has been so for Joan. At times a visit would find her chatty and engaged, *almost* as if she was back to her old self. Other times her family would notice that she still had a capacity for making connections, as if out of nowhere, and *it seemed as if* she had returned for a brief while. The disappointing part of these moments is that they were rare, brief, and unpredictable.

~

Six days before COVID changed the world, Joan was admitted to a Memory Care Unit in one of the buildings on the campus of her

Lifecare Facility. Remarkably, she survived what overcame others. Masks, social distancing, quarantines, and the fright that something like the Spanish Flu coming back. It all made no sense. Nothing remained the same.

Her family of five grown children, their spouses, partners, kids, and grandkids were steady in every way that could be imagined. Though Joan could not remember all the names (there are many) she remembered people and loved the feeling of family. She liked to hear about them all and smiled when she could make the connections. She did remember the names of her five kids but was always grateful for a helpful clue.

Over time, it became clearer that visits were best when they were shorter rather than extended. Gradually her family came to appreciate that though they could not give her memories or gifts as in years past, they could be present and provide moments, even knowing that those moments would not remain for her as memories.

~

Those who study and write of this disease have come to call it the long goodbye. That sounds poetic and soft, but it is neither of these. It is as if the love once shared is still there, but the person has begun an extended departure. Sometimes it feels as if the loved one has died, though she is still there. It is much harder on the family who stands watch than the person who slowly departs.

Joan has adjusted to this new reality as much as she is able. She is 94 and physically quite strong. The only path forward is for her family is to be present, to love kindly, and to affirm her value – which they steadily do. They can no longer give her memories, but they can give her moments. And for many of those moments, she smiles.

One more sentence brings it all the way home: Joan is my mother.

*"The Lord will watch your going out and your coming in
from this time forth, and even forever more."*
Psalm 121:8

. . . I Wonder . . .

*what will
become of me
when I relinquish,
the rev and the robe,
the distinction and the role?*

*So much
and so daily
these have been
one with me and in me,
such that the boundary lines*

*are on
the far side
of impossible to
discern any longer. Where
do I begin or, for that matter, end?*

*And how
complete has
the near-total eclipse
of my vocation hidden me
from the deeper nuances of my soul?*

*These aren't
small wonderings
as the voice of retirement*

*says, "You must let go
and trust who you will yet become.*

*The season of
life shifts later now,
just as the autumn breezes
unalterably remind the leaves
to surrender to an unknown path."*

One More Season

*Hard to fathom, five years gone —
in some ways short, others quite long.*

*I strain to bring your voice to ear
yet still, I find your presence near;
and wisdom's drift from high above
so many ways I've known your love.*

*The courage to live, the will to be,
the skills to set another free;
and passion for justice, ready to fire
with anger at times, sharp edges with ire.*

*Cool ocean breezes and Barnegat Bay,
an old affirmation, 'This is the day!'
Million-dollar views, fixing torn screens,
wondering deeply, stirring up dreams.*

*"Live toward fullness but never arrive,
grow 'til you die, don't merely survive.
So, centerboard down, sails full of Spirit,
reach into the wind, drift has no merit."*

*This all revealed in the gift of your being,
still opens my eyes to new ways of seeing.*[69]

---

[69] Written on the fifth anniversary of my father's death, July 21, 2015.

Heaven Only Knows

I want to dare the awesome ground of heaven with you. Even more, I'd like us to engage us in a theological frolic and do some wondering of the lofty sort. Every now and again that's a good thing to do: to try as we might to stretch the height and breadth and depth of our understanding – even to thoughts beyond our grasp.

Time magazine conducted a benchmark study about heaven that still holds its ground nearly 20 years later.[70] Among their questions were these. *Do you believe in the existence of heaven?* A whopping eighty-one percent of America said yes.

The research goes on to suggest that while heaven may not be a part of our daily conversations, most of us hold some notion, some image, some understanding of it in our lives, however vague or distant. It also affirms that "while most people still believe strongly in heaven, our concept for exactly what it is has grown quite foggy over time."

So, let's loosen up our spiritual imaginations. And, even if we're not in a heavenly mood, let's grant our hearts some altitude.

~

We begin with this truth: heaven meets each of us on *very* personal ground. For most of us such thoughts catch us at intensely personal times of loss or grief. They come to us as we seek to sort out one of life's most challenging experiences. As such, the notions we have of heaven are usually laden with multiple layers of individual belief and

---

[70] David VanBiema. "Does Heaven Exist?" in Time Magazine, March 24, 1997, pp. 77ff.

emotion. And, accordingly, the images that we conjure are the kind that need to be honored as expressions of the very personal and tender variety.

A nine-year-old boy had a near-death experience and tells us what he saw. "I dreamed I was with all the nuns and monks and nice animals. There were nice pigs and raccoons and giraffes. And all the nuns were there, too. And dogs, too. My brother was there and mom and dad. Cassidy was there. And my teachers were there. And the nuns and monks and my family and everybody else I love was there. And nice animals, too."[71] Isn't that beautiful?

A woman on her deathbed had an image of heaven that embraced an all-inclusive love. Her daughter said to her, "Mom, in heaven, everyone that we love is there." The mother, ever wiser, responded, "No, dear, in heaven we will love everyone who's there."

~

A second step in our thinking must eventually come to this realization. All that we might imagine about heaven falls far short of the whole truth. All our dreams, all our hunches, even what we might call convictions, are necessarily limited.

Paul confirms this: "Eye hath not seen, nor ear heard, the things which God hath prepared for them that love him."

The Bible is consistent in not being too definitive here. It only gives us metaphors and poetic hints. There's an image of a land of milk and honey. There's something called the promised land. There's comfort and welcome in a mansion with many rooms.

---

[71] Carol Zaleski. 'Picturing Paradise: When I Get to Heaven" in Christian Century, April 5, 2003, p. 31.

There's a vision of a new earth where tears are no more, and laughter and love and justice are all one. There's talk of a celestial city.

None of these is so definitive as to make us sure, for 'surety' and its close cousin 'certainty' make very misleading partners when it comes to matters of the spirit. Perhaps Robert Frost's wise words say it best: "Heaven gives its glimpses only to those not in a position to look too closely."[72]

~

A third thought. The scriptures help us to know that this realm called heaven begins on earth. It's not just about the hereafter; rather, it's also about the here and now. And, in fullness, it can be experienced as God's realm that is both in this moment and in a promise to come.

Jesus taught us this. He said, "the realm of God is within you," "the realm of God is at hand," "you are very near to the realm of God," and a moment later he also said, "I go to prepare a place for you," "I will not leave you bereft," and "lo I am with you always."

In whatever way we wrestle these through, they bear the mark of paradox and mystery. Paradox as the not-yet is already; and mystery as the world right here also bears a dimension of the beyond.

~

A last thought. No matter how we might interpret heaven in the scriptures or in life, it's ultimately about things being whole and at home with God. In the words of the poet, it's about all manner of things being well. Love and peace and joy and harmony and justice and eternity all in one. All of these are a far beneath and beyond our

---

[72] "A Passing Glimpse" in Christian Century, October 23, 2002, p. 10.

more earthly and earth-bound lives, and in ways ineffable, deep in the heart of the One whom we call God.

You may recall the name of Cardinal Bernardin. He was a Catholic priest whose journey with cancer took him to some very tender places. He wrote these words shortly before he died. "Now that I am getting near to death many people have asked me to tell them about heaven. I sometimes smile at the request because I don't know any more than they do. Yet one man asked me if I looked forward to being united with God and all who have gone before me. In answering I made a connection to the first time that I traveled with my mother and sister to my parent's homeland in northern Italy. Oddly, though I had never been there, I felt as if I was very much at home when I arrived, like I had somehow been there before. After years of looking through my mother's photo albums, I knew the mountains, the land, the houses, the people. As soon as we entered the valley I said, 'My God, I know this place. I am home.' Somehow, I think crossing from this life into heaven will be just like this. I will finally be home."[73]

~

May our horizons be stretched by these thoughts. May they encourage us to live fully the moments that we are given now. May they assure us with the realm beneath and beyond all that we can name or understand. And may they bring us to rest in the name and spirit of the God whose realm is so vast that heaven and earth are ever together held as one – in mystery, and in paradox, and in love.

"You are not far from the kingdom of God." Mark 12: 34

---

[73] Cardinal Joseph Bernardin. The Gift of Peace. Image Books, 1998.

A Smaller World

A visit to an extended care facility for "Active Aging" is on my mind. An old friend and I sat in the spaciousness of an Atrium, which is where he preferred to entertain those who dropped by to see him.

He got right to what was on his mind and just waiting for a listener. "My world is getting smaller," he confided. "It's hard to explain. A lost word, a thought on the edge of a sentence that just seems to fall out of my mind. No matter what I try to do I can't retrieve it."

"I find myself bereft in the middle of conversations, though I'm not sure that anyone else is aware how much I drift. I am still quick enough to cover for the gaps. Usually that is. Or at least I think so. But it's an awful feeling."

"I once was quite agile at engaging others, fast on my feet, accomplished with words. Nimble in thinking and speaking. Socially adept. Able to know and remember who I am talking with. Now those skills are falling away."

A bit of silence grew in between us, and then he went on. "Did you hear that I gave up driving? Truthfully, I had to do that. I was having too many near misses, and hurting myself I could stand, but hurting or killing another person – I would never forgive myself."

"The sweet part of all of this is that I have found comfort in just being here now and in much simpler pleasures. A good nap is worth a lot to me. An old book read again, received with new insights. Quiet visits with friends."

"More tea and less coffee are a nice change, too. It feels good to let go of my former need to perform. I'm finding that conversations with one or two people at a time rather than many all at once are so much more manageable."

"And safety. I feel safe here. I like the people. I never thought I would say that about a place like this. Our apartment is comfortable. My wife and I can manage so much easier than before. It's nice not to worry about cooking our main meal each day or cleaning up."

An appreciative pause grew into the space between us. "Thanks for coming by. I guess dominated the whole visit with my own chatter again," he said apologetically. "I like to listen, and to hear how things are for you makes my heart very full. I'll be back soon," I promised. "I'll look forward to that," he said.

But our time was not to be again. Though we talked several times on the phone arranging for a subsequent time to come, he took a quick turn and died before another visit. Perhaps someday, in the mystery of it all, we'll pick it up again on the other side.

"Teach us to number our days that we might gain a heart of wisdom."
Psalm 90:12

Mortality

*I stood on fresh earth today,
laying to rest a dear departed woman
of ninety-three years.*

*The eyes of her widower,
older yet, were pensive and hungry
as he watched my lips move.*

*I spoke with the assurance of the ages:
"earth to earth, ashes to ashes,
dust to dust is our way of going home."*

*How haunting it is to wonder
and yet not to know what will be
in that twinkling of an eye -*

*when the trumpet sounds
and deep gladness is all around
as heaven is revealed in plain sight.*

*This we all know: We will die.
But this we do not know: What will yet be.
Thanks be to God: (I think).*

The Owl's Call

*The song of an owl startled me to waking,
filling up the deep end of the wee hours.*

*Hauntingly beautiful to the break of day,
and beautifully haunting, too.*

*Somewhere lying between the dark and the dawn
I remembered a book's title, an archetypal story:*

*"I Heard the Owl Call My Name."
It was steeped in mystical wisdom,*

*the owl being the harbinger of death
naming the next to cross over rivers and skies*

*to something more and far beyond
the thin veil masking the edge.*

*But who's name did I hear?
Was it mine, or one nearby whom I love?*

*Or was it only a song reminding me
that one day the time of awakening will be over.*

About the Author

Geordie Campbell retired in 2020 following a beloved vocation as a Pastor in the United Church of Christ. He smiles playfully as he calls *almost* all of those years fulfilling and enchanting!

His educational credits include Susquehanna University (BA, 1975); Andover Newton Theological School (MDiv, 1980); and Hartford Seminary (DMin 1992). He is an alum of the Spiritual Life Center in West Hartford, CT where he learned the art of Spiritual Direction; and of Auburn Seminary in NYC where he was trained in Executive Coaching.

He has served in four settings: Trinitarian Congregational Church in Concord, MA; Newfane Congregational Church in Newfane, VT; South Congregational Church in Granby, CT; and First Church of Christ Congregational in West Hartford, CT. As he retired from a 15-year tenure at his last post he was granted the honorary title of Pastor Emeritus.

He and his wife Pam have two grown children and one grandchild. They are delighted to be living along the southern coast of Maine with their shih tzu companion, Laddie.

Ordering Information

Copies of *That You May Become ~ Living into Faith* are available by direct order from:

> Geordie Campbell
> 55 Creeks Edge Drive
> Saco, ME 04072
> 860-878-4197
> cgc.pastor.emeritus@gmail.com
>
> Single copy: $12.50
> Shipping: $ 5.00

Also available at the same address and cost are copies of his earlier book *Tell Me with a Story ~ Narrative Prompts for Spiritual Seekers.*